Journey to Transformative Lent

A 40-Day Lenten Guide to Prayer, Reflection, and Renewal

William Gomes

Journey to Transformative Lent: A 40-Day Lenten Guide to Prayer, Reflection, and Renewal
Copyright © 2023 William Gomes

All rights reserved. No part of this publication may be reproduced or transmitted in any form or by any means, electronic or mechanical, including photocopying, recording, or any information storage or retrieval system, without prior permission in writing from the publishers.

ISBN: 9798390610664

Cover designed by: Geeth Kalhara

Typeset by: Tariq Khan

Table of Contents

Introduction 5
Day 1: Beginning with Gratitude 7
Day 2: Seeking Forgiveness 10
Day 3: Cultivating Humility 13
Day 4: Compassion for Others 18
Day 5: Living in the Present Moment 21
Day 6: Encountering Jesus in Others 24
Day 7: Understanding Fasting and Abstinence 27
Day 8: Developing Patience 30
Day 9: Deepening Your Prayer Life 33
Day 10: Embracing Almsgiving and Generosity 36
Day 11: Cultivating a Heart of Joy 39
Day 12: Walking with Mary, Mother of Jesus 43
Day 13: The Power of Silence 46
Day 14: Building Community and Fellowship 49
Day 15: Encountering God in Nature 53
Day 16: Trusting in God's Providence 59
Day 17: The Practice of Discernment 62
Day 18: Cultivating a Servant's Heart 67
Day 19: The Role of Suffering in Spiritual Growth 71
Day 20: The Beauty of God's Mercy 76
Day 21: Nurturing Spiritual Friendships 81
Day 22: Recognising God's Love 85
Day 23: The Power of the Eucharist 89
Day 24: The Call to Evangelisation 92
Day 25: Practicing Gratitude in All Circumstances 97
Day 26: Embracing the Beatitudes 101

Day 27: The Gift of Hope 105
Day 28: The Example of the Saints 109
Day 29: Living a Life of Simplicity 113
Day 30: Cultivating the Virtue of Temperance 117
Day 31: The Spiritual Works of Mercy 121
Day 32: The Importance of Spiritual Reading 125
Day 33: The Power of Intercessory Prayer 129
Day 34: The Call to Holiness 133
Day 35: The Power of Forgiveness 137
Day 36: The Gift of Faith 141
Day 37: The Fruit of the Spirit 145
Day 38: The Joy of Serving Others 149
Day 39: Preparing for the Resurrection 153
Day 40: Celebrating New Life in Christ 156

Introduction

"Journey to Transformative Lent: A 40-Day Lenten Guide to Prayer, Reflection, and Renewal" is an essential guide to spiritual transformation during the season of Lent. Written by renowned spiritual writer, human rights activist, and freelance journalist William Gomes, this book offers readers a unique and transformative experience through prayer, reflection, and renewal.

As readers embark on a 40-day journey of personal and spiritual growth, they will find practical guidance and insights to deepen their prayer life, reflect on their relationship with God, and renew their commitment to living a more faithful and fulfilling life. Unlike other Lenten devotionals, the author takes a unique approach by weaving together biblical teachings, prayers, and practical exercises to create a deeply engaging and transformative experience.

Readers can expect a comprehensive guide that leads them on a transformative journey of self-reflection and examination. The book includes daily readings and reflections for each of the 40 days of Lent, along with practical exercises and actions to apply the teachings to daily life. These exercises are designed to help readers connect with God and deepen their relationship with Him.

One of the book's unique features is that it offers practical ways to apply the teachings to daily life. Each day includes actions that readers can take to put the teachings into practice and transform their lives. These actions are designed to be simple yet powerful and will help readers experience real growth and transformation.

By the end of the 40-day journey, readers will have developed a deeper understanding of themselves, their relationship with God, and their role in the world. They will have explored a wide range of spiritual practices, including prayer, fasting, contemplation, and service, and will have gained new insights into the meaning and purpose of the Lenten season. Most importantly, readers will have developed a spiritual toolkit that they can use throughout the year to deepen their faith and live more fulfilling lives.

This book is a transforming and life-changing guide to prayer, reflection, and renewal. It provides readers with a roadmap for deepening their spiritual practice and transforming their lives. It is not a book that tells readers what to do but provides them with the tools and resources they need to explore their spiritual journey in a meaningful and transformative way.

Overall, "Journey to Transformative Lent: A 40-Day Lenten Guide to Prayer, Reflection, and Renewal" is a must-read for anyone seeking to deepen their spiritual practice and experience true transformation during the Lenten season. It is a comprehensive resource that offers practical guidance and inspiration for anyone seeking to deepen their spiritual practice and transform their life. By providing a structured 40-day journey, the book allows readers to fully immerse themselves in the Lenten season and experience the transformation that comes from intentional reflection and prayer.

Day 1: Beginning with Gratitude

As we embark on this sacred journey together, let us start by cultivating a heart filled with gratitude. When we focus on the blessings and gifts in our lives, our hearts open to God's love and we become more aware of His presence. This first day of our 40-day Lenten journey invites us to pause and give thanks for the many ways God has blessed us.

Prayer:

St. Ignatius' Prayer for Generosity

Lord, teach me to be generous.

Teach me to serve you as you deserve;

To give and not to count the cost,

To fight and not to heed the wounds,

To toil and not to seek for rest,

To labour and not to ask for reward,

To give of myself and not ask for a reward,

Except the reward of knowing that I am doing your will.

St. Ignatius of Loyola, Pray for us.

Amen

Reflection:

Take a moment to consider the many blessings in your life. From the people you love to the opportunities you've been given, there is so much to be grateful for. As you reflect on these gifts, remember that they are not only expressions of God's love for you but also invitations to respond with gratitude and generosity.

Questions:

- What are three things you are grateful for today?
  - Lesley's phone call, when we caught up
  - the opportunity to start Lent by taking part in the Mass
  - the glorious weather and the visible renewal of the earth.

- How can you express your gratitude to God for these blessings?
  - remembering friends in prayer
  - regular worship
  - praising Him for his gifts in nature.

- In what ways can you share your blessings with others?
  - more mindful and active with friends.
  - supportive

Action:

Write a thank-you note to someone who has positively impacted your life. This simple act of gratitude can help you to recognise the blessings in your life and remind you of the importance of expressing appreciation to those who have made a difference.

As we close this first day of our Lenten journey, let us carry with us a spirit of gratitude. May our hearts be filled with thankfulness for the many ways God has blessed us, and may this gratitude inspire us to be generous in our service to others. As we look forward to the days ahead, let us continue to seek opportunities to express our gratitude and grow closer to God.

Day 2: Seeking Forgiveness

On this second day of our Lenten journey, we turn our attention to the theme of forgiveness. Forgiveness is a powerful force that can bring healing and freedom to our lives. As we seek to grow in our relationship with God, it is essential that we also seek forgiveness and reconciliation with others.

Prayer:

The Parable of the Prodigal Son (Luke 15:11-32)

Take a few moments to read and reflect on the Parable of the Prodigal Son from the Gospel of Luke. As you read this powerful story, consider the themes of forgiveness, mercy, and reconciliation at its heart.

Reflection:

The power of forgiveness is immense; it can transform relationships, heal wounds, and bring about a sense of inner peace. As we journey through Lent, it is essential to examine our hearts and seek forgiveness from those we have wronged, as well as extend forgiveness to those who have hurt us. In doing so, we open ourselves up to the healing power of God's love and mercy.

Questions:

- Is there someone you need to forgive or ask for forgiveness from?

- How does holding onto resentment impact your spiritual life?

  Stultifies it, occupies mental space and physical stress.

- What steps can you take to seek reconciliation and healing in your relationships?

Action:

Seek forgiveness from someone you have wronged or forgive someone who has hurt you. This may be as simple as a heartfelt conversation or a written apology, or it may involve a more involved process of healing and reconciliation. Whatever the situation, remember that forgiveness is a gift we give to ourselves as much as to the other person.

As we continue our Lenten journey, let us remember the importance of forgiveness and reconciliation in our spiritual lives. May we be willing to seek forgiveness from those we have hurt and extend forgiveness to those who have wounded us. In doing so, we open ourselves up to the healing power of God's love and mercy and take another step closer to Him on our journey. Let us carry this spirit of forgiveness with us as we move forward into the days ahead.

Day 3: Cultivating Humility

On this third day of our Lenten journey, we focus on the virtue of humility. Humility helps us recognise our strengths and weaknesses and fosters an attitude of openness to God's grace. As we seek to grow spiritually, cultivating humility enables us to become more attuned to the divine guidance and love present in our lives.

Prayer:

The Litany of Humility by Rafael Cardinal Merry del Val

O Jesus, meek and humble of heart,

Hear me.

From the desire of being esteemed,

Deliver me, O Jesus.

From the desire of being loved,

Deliver me, O Jesus.

From the desire of being extolled,

Deliver me, O Jesus.

From the desire of being honoured,

Deliver me, O Jesus.

From the desire of being praised,

Deliver me, O Jesus.

From the desire of being preferred to others,

Deliver me, O Jesus.

From the desire of being consulted,
Deliver me, O Jesus.
From the desire of being approved,
Deliver me, O Jesus.
From the fear of being humiliated,
Deliver me, O Jesus.
From the fear of being despised,
Deliver me, O Jesus.
From the fear of suffering rebukes,
Deliver me, O Jesus.
From the fear of being calumniated,
Deliver me, O Jesus.
From the fear of being forgotten,
Deliver me, O Jesus.
From the fear of being ridiculed,
Deliver me, O Jesus.
From the fear of being wronged,
Deliver me, O Jesus.
From the fear of being suspected,
Deliver me, O Jesus.
That others may be loved more than I,
Jesus, grant me the grace to desire it.

That others may be esteemed more than I,

Jesus, grant me the grace to desire it.

That, in the opinion of the world, others may increase and I may decrease,

Jesus, grant me the grace to desire it.

That others may be chosen, and I set aside,

Jesus, grant me the grace to desire it.

That others may be praised and I unnoticed,

Jesus, grant me the grace to desire it.

That others may be preferred to me in everything,

Jesus, grant me the grace to desire it.

That others may become holier than I, provided that I may become as holy as I should,

Jesus, grant me the grace to desire it.

Amen.

Reflection:

Humility is a virtue that helps us see ourselves as we truly are, with all our strengths and weaknesses. It allows us to be honest with ourselves and to recognize our need for God's grace in our lives. As we cultivate humility, we become more receptive to the guidance and wisdom that God offers us on our spiritual journey.

Questions:

- How does humility help you grow spiritually?

  - Less of self, more of others
  - To follow the example of Jesus

- In what ways can you practise humility in your daily life?

  - Not seeking the limelight
  - To listen more and speak less

- What steps can you take to cultivate humility in your relationships with others?

  - To be less controlling - my ways and ideas are not always right.

In the space provided above, write your answers and reflections on these suggestions. Remember, this is a personal journey, and your responses will help you grow and deepen your understanding of the importance of spiritual reading in your spiritual life.

Action:

Perform an act of service for someone in need without expecting recognition. This could be something small, like holding the door for someone or offering a kind word, or something more involved, like volunteering your time or resources. The goal is to practice humility by serving others without seeking praise or acknowledgement.

As we continue our Lenten journey, let us strive to cultivate the virtue of humility in our lives. By recognizing our strengths and weaknesses, we open ourselves up to the grace and guidance that God has to offer. May we approach each day with a humble heart, ready to learn, grow, and serve in whatever ways we are called. Let this spirit of humility accompany us as we journey onward towards the days ahead.

Day 4: Compassion for Others

As we journey through Lent, let us turn our attention to the importance of compassion in our lives. Compassion is the ability to empathize with and understand the suffering of others, and it is a crucial aspect of our spiritual growth. By cultivating compassion, we become more Christ-like in our thoughts, words, and actions.

Prayer:

St. Francis of Assisi's Prayer for Peace

Lord, make me an instrument of Your peace;

Where there is hatred, let me sow love;

where there is injury, pardon;

where there is doubt, faith;

where there is despair, hope;

where there is darkness, light;

where there is sadness, joy.

O Divine Master, grant that I may not so much seek

to be consoled as to console;

to be understood as to understand;

to be loved as to love.

For it is in giving that we receive,

it is in pardoning that we are pardoned,

and it is in dying that we are born to eternal life.

Amen.

Reflection:

Empathy and understanding are essential components of compassion. As we grow in our spiritual lives, it is important to develop the ability to see the world from another's perspective and to feel their pain as if it were our own. This ability to empathize with others allows us to extend love and kindness in our relationships, helping to create a more compassionate world.

Questions:

❖ How can you cultivate compassion for others?

By (trying to) look at others as Jesus did - and with gentle kindness

❖ In what ways have you experienced compassion from others?

Generosity of spirit from Lesley (both), friends who have listened to me

❖ How can compassion transform your relationships and the world around you?

By being kind to those who struggle, and those I find uncongenial or difficult. By being non-judgmental.

✓ Action:

Donate to a charity or volunteer at a local community centre. As you give your time, resources, or energy to help others, you will be practising compassion and making a positive impact on the lives of those in need.

As we continue on our Lenten journey, let us strive to cultivate compassion for others in our thoughts, words, and actions. By empathizing with the suffering of others and seeking to alleviate their pain, we become more Christ-like and contribute to the healing and transformation of our world. May the spirit of compassion guide us as we journey onward towards the days ahead.

Day 5: Living in the Present Moment

As we embark on the fifth day of our Lenten journey, it is crucial to pause and reflect on the importance of living in the present moment. In our fast-paced world, it is all too easy to become preoccupied with the future or dwell on the past. However, by learning to embrace the present moment, we can become more attuned to God's presence and guidance in our lives. Our connection with the divine deepens when we are fully present and open to receiving the grace that God bestows upon us in each moment.

Prayer:

Prayer of Detachment

O God, rid me of myself

And place me wholly in You.

Let nothing remain of me but what is Yours,

And let me live in You alone.

Amen.

Reflection:

Embracing the present moment means learning to let go of anxiety about the future and being fully present with the grace and guidance that God offers us right now. When we allow ourselves to be consumed by worry, we miss the opportunity to experience the fullness of God's love and presence. By living in the present, we can deepen our relationship with God and become more attuned to the divine presence in our lives.

Questions:

❖ How can living in the present moment deepen your relationship with God?

Becomes easier to hold the present moment, and give it to Him and receive His Spirit of grace

❖ What steps can you take to let go of worry and embrace the present?

Visualise the laying down of a fear or worry at the foot of the Cross or the open tomb and leaving it there.

❖ How can you practise mindfulness in your daily life to remain present and open to God's grace?

By steadily recalling a wandering or chattering inner voice

Action:

Consider spending 10 minutes in silence, focusing on your breath and being present. As thoughts or worries arise, gently bring your focus back to your breath and the present moment. This practice can help to still your mind and open your heart to the divine presence in your life. Remember, this is only a suggestion, and you may choose a different approach that resonates with you.

As we continue on our Lenten journey, let us strive to live in the present moment and be open to the grace that God has to offer us each day. By letting go of worry and anxiety about the future, we can deepen our relationship with God and become more attuned to the divine presence in our lives. We have come far in our journey, and as we move forward, let us be mindful of the progress we have made and the growth that is yet to come. May this spirit of mindfulness accompany us as we journey onward towards the days ahead, remaining present and open to God's love and guidance.

Day 6: Encountering Jesus in Others

As we journey through Lent, one of the most transformative aspects of our spiritual growth is learning to see the face of Christ in those around us, especially the marginalised and those in need. It is often said that Christ is present in the least of our brothers and sisters, and it is through our interactions with them that we encounter the divine. On this sixth day of our Lenten journey, we will explore how we can recognise Jesus in the people around us and how we can better serve those in need.

Prayer:

Lord, help me to see Your face

In the distressing disguise of the poor.

Teach me to recognise You

In the hungry, the homeless, and the broken.

May I never tire of serving You

In the least of my brothers and sisters.

Amen.

Reflection:

As followers of Christ, we are called to recognise the divine presence in everyone we encounter, especially those who are marginalised or struggling. By seeing Jesus in the faces of those around us, we can develop a deeper sense of empathy and understanding, helping to break down the barriers that divide us. As we learn to see Christ in others, we are also called to serve them, responding to their needs with love and compassion.

Questions:

❖ How can you see Jesus in the people around you?

To use His eyes to see them and their needs.

❖ How can you better serve those in need?

By drawing closer to them and listening to discern their needs.

❖ In what ways can recognising the face of Christ in others transform your relationships and your spiritual life?

A strengthening of recognising our common humanity and sharing God's grace.

In the space provided above, write your answers and reflections on these suggestions. Remember, this is a personal journey, and your responses will help you grow and deepen your understanding of the importance of spiritual reading in your spiritual life.

Action:

You might consider sharing a meal or conversation with someone lonely or marginalised. By reaching out to those in need, we not only provide comfort and support and the opportunity to encounter Jesus in a profound way. This is just a suggestion, and you may choose a different approach that resonates with you and aligns with your circumstances.

As we continue on our Lenten journey, let us strive to encounter Jesus in the faces of those around us, especially the marginalised and those in need. By recognising the divine presence in others and serving them with love and compassion, we can experience spiritual growth and transformation. We have come far in our journey, and as we move forward, let us be mindful of the progress we have made and the growth that is yet to come. May the spirit of Christ-like love and service accompany us as we journey onward towards the days ahead, encountering the divine in the faces of those we meet along the way.

Day 7: Understanding Fasting and Abstinence

As we reach the seventh day of our Lenten journey, it is essential to pause and reflect on the spiritual significance of fasting and abstinence during this holy season. These practices have long been a central part of the Lenten experience, helping us to grow closer to God by letting go of our attachments to worldly pleasures and distractions. By embracing fasting and abstinence, we can cultivate discipline, focus, and a deeper sense of humility, all of which can strengthen our relationship with God.

Prayer:

Heavenly Father,

Grant us the grace to live this Lenten season

With renewed hearts and minds.

May our fasting and abstinence

Draw us closer to You and our brothers and sisters in need.

Help us to recognize the blessings You bestow upon us

And to share them generously with others.

Amen.

Reflection:

Fasting and abstinence are spiritual practices that have been a part of the Christian tradition for centuries. During Lent, these practices help us to grow in our relationship with God by letting go of our attachments to worldly pleasures and distractions. Through fasting and abstinence, we can develop discipline, focus, and a deeper sense of humility, which can bring us closer to God and help us become more aware of our spiritual needs.

Questions:

- What are your intentions for fasting and abstinence during Lent?

  Not to spend money on myself, unless strictly necessary.

- How can these practices strengthen your relationship with God?

  ?

- What are some ways you can incorporate fasting and abstinence into your daily life during Lent?

Action:

Consider abstaining from a luxury or habit during Lent to cultivate discipline and focus. This act can help you grow in your relationship with God and create space for spiritual growth. Remember that this is a suggestion; you may choose a different approach that resonates with you and aligns with your circumstances.

As we continue on our Lenten journey, let us embrace the spiritual significance of fasting and abstinence as a means of deepening our relationship with God. By cultivating discipline, focus, and humility through these practices, we can grow in our spiritual lives and become more open to the presence and guidance of the divine. We have come far in our journey, and as we move forward, let us be mindful of the progress we have made and the growth that is yet to come. May the spirit of fasting and abstinence accompany us as we journey onward towards the days ahead, seeking a deeper connection with God and a greater understanding of our spiritual needs.

Day 8: Developing Patience

As we progress in our Lenten journey, it is crucial to consider the importance of cultivating patience in our lives. Patience is a virtue that can profoundly impact our spiritual growth and relationships with others. In a world that often rewards instant gratification and quick results, embracing patience can be challenging. However, by overcoming impatience and learning to face life's challenges with grace, we can deepen our relationship with God and better navigate the ups and downs of life.

Prayer:

Lord, teach me to be patient,

With life, with people, and with myself.

Help me to accept the things I cannot change,

And to trust in Your perfect timing.

Grant me the wisdom to know

That all things work together for good,

And the strength to persevere in faith.

Amen.

Reflection:

Developing patience is an essential aspect of our spiritual growth. Impatience can lead to frustration, stress, and strained relationships with others. By cultivating patience, we can face life's challenges with grace and an open heart, allowing us to grow closer to God and become more aware of His presence in our lives. As we develop patience, we can better navigate the ups and downs of life and experience a more profound sense of peace and contentment.

Questions:

❖ How does impatience affect your spiritual life?

Jangles my senses, churns up my mind and causes an abrupt lack of self-control.

❖ What strategies can you use to develop patience?

To breathe and to become more aware of the triggers and consequences of impatience.

❖ How might cultivating patience improve your relationships with others and your relationship with God?

Family life would be more peaceful, and I would be more at peace with God.

In the space provided below, write your answers and reflections on these suggestions. Remember, this is a personal journey, and your responses will help you grow and deepen your understanding of the importance of spiritual reading in your spiritual life.

Action:

You may want to practice patience with someone who typically tests your limits. By doing so, you can gain valuable insights into your reactions and grow in your ability to remain calm and centred in challenging situations. Remember that this is a suggestion; you may choose a different approach that resonates with you and aligns with your circumstances.

As we continue our Lenten journey, let us strive to develop patience, facing life's challenges with grace and an open heart. By cultivating this essential virtue, we can deepen our relationship with God and improve our interactions with others. We have come far in our journey, and as we move forward, let us be mindful of the progress we have made and the growth that is yet to come. May the spirit of patience accompany us as we journey onward towards the days ahead, helping us to navigate the ups and downs of life with grace and wisdom.

Day 9: Deepening Your Prayer Life

As we journey through Lent, it is essential to focus on the role of prayer in our spiritual lives. Prayer is our lifeline to God, an intimate conversation that helps us grow closer to Him and strengthen our faith. Yet, many of us may find that our prayer lives can become stagnant, repetitive, or lack the depth we desire. Today, let us explore ways to deepen our connection with God through prayer, revitalizing our spiritual lives and enriching our relationship with our Creator.

Prayer:

St. John Vianney's Prayer to Jesus

I love You, O my God,

and my only desire is to love You

Until the last breath of my life.

I love You, O my infinitely lovable God,

And I prefer to die loving You,

than to live without loving You.

I love You, Lord and the only grace I ask is to love You eternally.

My God, if my tongue cannot say in every moment that I love You,

I want my heart to repeat it to You as often as I draw breath.

Amen.

Reflection:

Deepening our prayer life is vital for our spiritual journey. Prayer helps us to connect with God, discern His will for our lives, and find solace in times of need. By enhancing our prayer life, we can experience a more profound sense of God's presence and develop a closer relationship with Him. As we seek to deepen our prayer life, we should explore new forms of prayer and meditation, creating a more enriching and fulfilling experience in our conversations with God.

Questions:

- How does prayer help you in your spiritual journey?

  Not at present — I don't know how to pray effectively — but what does that mean?

- What are some ways you can enhance your prayer life?

  By setting aside a time — when? — to pray — and starting with verbalising silently.

- How can deepening your prayer life impact your relationship with God and others?

Action:

You might want to dedicate an additional 15 minutes to prayer today, trying a new form of prayer or meditation. This could include contemplative prayer, Lectio Divina, or the practice of mindfulness. Remember that this is a suggestion; you may choose a different approach that resonates with you and aligns with your circumstances.

As we move forward in our Lenten journey, let us be intentional in deepening our prayer lives and strengthening our connection with God. By exploring new ways to pray and dedicating more time to our conversations with our Creator, we can experience a more profound sense of His presence and guidance in our lives. We have come a long way on this journey, and as we continue, let us be mindful of the progress we have made and the growth that is yet to come. May our prayers serve as a guiding light, leading us closer to God and enriching our spiritual lives.

Day 10: Embracing Almsgiving and Generosity

As we continue our Lenten journey, one of the core practices that we are called to embrace is almsgiving. Almsgiving is the act of giving to others, particularly those in need, without expecting anything in return. This selfless act of generosity not only benefits the recipient but also enriches our own spiritual lives. By engaging in acts of kindness and generosity, we open our hearts to God's grace and love, which in turn, allows us to grow closer to Him. Today, let us reflect on the spiritual benefits of almsgiving and explore ways we can practice generosity in our daily lives.

Prayer:

St. Ignatius' Prayer for Generosity

Lord Jesus, teach me to be generous.
Teach me to serve as you deserve,
To give and not to count the cost,
To fight and not to heed the wounds,
To labor and not to seek to rest,
To give of my self and not ask for a reward,

Except the reward of knowing that I am doing your will.

St. Ignatius of Loyola, Pray for us.

Amen

Reflection:

The practice of almsgiving and generosity is a way for us to demonstrate our love for God and our neighbours. By giving without expecting anything in return, we can detach ourselves from material possessions and focus on the spiritual riches that come from a loving and generous heart. Additionally, almsgiving helps us to develop empathy and compassion for others, allowing us to see Christ in each person we encounter. As we engage in acts of generosity, we not only help those in need but also open ourselves up to the transforming power of God's grace and love.

Questions:

- How can you practice generosity in your daily life?

    - To give freely, without reservation.

- What are some ways you've experienced generosity from others?

    - Tamara's mother making exquisite quilts for me
    - Jane's generosity

- How does practising generosity impact your relationship with God and others?

    Detachment from "things", compassion and empathy

In the space provided below, write your answers and reflections on these suggestions. Remember, this is a personal journey, and your responses will help you grow and deepen your understanding of the importance of spiritual reading in your spiritual life.

_____

_____

_____

_____

_____

_____

Action:

You may want to consider donating items or money to a charity or someone in need. This could be a local food bank, a homeless shelter, or an individual you know who is struggling. Remember that this is a suggestion; you can choose a different approach that resonates with you and aligns with your circumstances.

As we continue our Lenten journey, let us remember the importance of embracing almsgiving and generosity as a means of growing closer to God and our fellow human beings. By giving without expectation, we can experience the spiritual benefits of detachment, compassion, and empathy. As we strive to be more generous and selfless in our daily lives, we will see the transformative power of God's grace at work within us. Let us be encouraged by how far we have come on this journey and look forward to the growth and transformation that lies ahead. May our acts of generosity be a testament to our faith and a reflection of God's love at work in our lives.

Day 11: Cultivating a Heart of Joy

As we continue our Lenten journey today, we turn our focus towards cultivating a heart of joy. Joy is a profound and deep sense of contentment that arises from a close relationship with God, even amid suffering and challenging circumstances. It is essential to recognise that joy is not the same as happiness, which can be fleeting and dependent on external factors. Instead, joy is a spiritual gift that sustains us, even in our darkest moments. As we walk through this day, let us explore how we can nurture a heart of joy and learn to find solace in God's presence, regardless of the trials we may face.

Prayer:

St. Philip Neri's Prayer for Joy

O Holy Saint Philip Neri, Patron Saint of Joy,
you who trusted Scripture's promise that the Lord is always at hand, and
that we need not have anxiety about anything:
in your compassion heal our worries and sorrows,
and lift the burdens from our hearts.
We come to you as one whose heart swells with abundant love for God and
all creation.
Hear us we pray, especially in this need: (make request here)
Keep us safe through your loving intercession
and may the joy of the Holy Spirit which filled your heart,
Saint Philip,
transform our lives and bring us peace.

Amen.

Reflection:

Amid life's challenges and suffering, it can be difficult to find joy. Yet, the beauty of our faith is that God's presence remains with us in all situations, even when we feel overwhelmed or abandoned. The key to cultivating a heart of joy is recognising and embracing God's constant presence in our lives. By doing so, we can learn to find solace in His love and comfort, even when our circumstances seem bleak.

As we reflect on the role of joy in our spiritual growth, it is essential to remember that joy is not a denial of pain or suffering. Instead, joy is the result of a deep and abiding trust in God's love and providence. When we choose to find joy amid our struggles, we open ourselves to the grace and peace that God offers, allowing His love to transform our hearts and minds. Through this transformation, we can become more resilient and better equipped to face the challenges that life presents, knowing that we are never alone in our journey.

Questions:

❖ How can you find joy even in difficult circumstances?

By turning to the Lord when things and people overwhelm.

❖ How does joy affect your spiritual growth?

When I don't feel at peace

In the space provided below, write your answers and reflections on these suggestions. Remember, this is a personal journey, and your responses will help you grow and deepen your understanding of the importance of spiritual reading in your spiritual life.

_____
_____
_____
_____
_____
_____

Action:

Consider the following suggestions inspired by Catholic social teachings as ways to spread joy to those around you:

❖ Share a kind word or compliment with someone you encounter today.

❖ Offer help to a neighbour or a member of your community who may be struggling.

❖ Pray for those who are suffering in your community or around the world.

❖ Engage in acts of solidarity by supporting local businesses or advocating for social justice issues.

❖ Donate to a charity that focuses on alleviating poverty and suffering, both locally and globally.

❖ Remember that these suggestions are meant to inspire you and are not mandatory.

❖ Choose the actions that resonate with you and align with your circumstances.

As we journey through this Lenten season, let us continue to cultivate a heart of joy, trusting in God's presence and love, even when faced with challenges and suffering. By learning to find joy in all circumstances, we open ourselves to the transformative power of God's grace and love. As we grow in our spiritual lives and deepen our relationship with God, we become more resilient and able to face life's challenges with courage and faith.

As we come to the end of Day 11, let us look back on our journey so far with gratitude and humility, recognising the progress we've made and the grace that has sustained us. Each day is an opportunity to grow closer to God and deepen our understanding of His love and mercy. Let us carry the lessons we've learned into tomorrow and the days to come, trusting that our efforts to cultivate a heart of joy will not be in vain.

Tomorrow, we will explore another aspect of our spiritual journey, but for now, take some time to reflect on the joy that God has placed within your heart. Remember, it is through our trials and tribulations that we can truly experience the depth of God's love and the gift of joy that He offers us. May your heart be filled with the joy of the Lord, and may it radiate to those around you, transforming not only your life but the lives of others as well.

May God bless you and keep you on this journey, and may you always find joy in His presence.

Day 12: Walking with Mary, Mother of Jesus

Welcome to Day 12 of our transformative Lenten journey. So far, we have explored various aspects of our spiritual growth, and today, we will turn our focus to Mary, the Mother of Jesus. Mary's unwavering faith and obedience to God's will serve as an inspiring example for all Christians. As we walk with Mary today, let us open our hearts and minds to learn from her example and deepen our relationship with her.

Mary was a young woman who, when faced with the extraordinary and challenging task of becoming the mother of the Son of God, said yes with courage and trust. Her "fiat," her willingness to accept God's plan for her life, is a powerful example of faith and surrender to the divine will. Through her life, Mary teaches us how to be open to God's call, embrace His plan for us, and persevere through the hardships and uncertainties we may face.

Reflection:

Mary's journey was not an easy one. From the moment of the Annunciation, when the angel Gabriel announced that she would give birth to the Messiah, Mary faced numerous challenges. Yet, through it all, she remained steadfast in her faith, trusting in God's plan even when it seemed impossible. Her life was marked by sorrow, particularly as she witnessed the suffering and death of her beloved son, Jesus. However, Mary's faith never wavered, and she continued to believe in God's promises.

As Christians, we are called to follow Mary's example of faith, humility, and obedience. In our own spiritual journey, we may face challenges and difficulties that test our faith. Like Mary, we must trust in God's plan even when it is difficult to understand or accept. We must also learn to surrender our will to God, knowing that His ways are higher than our ways and that He has a purpose for every trial we face.

In addition to her unwavering faith, Mary also serves as a powerful intercessor for us. As the mother of Jesus and our spiritual mother, she is uniquely positioned to bring our prayers and petitions before her son.

Through her intercession, we can draw closer to Jesus and grow in our relationship with Him.

Questions:

❖ How can you learn from Mary's example in your own spiritual journey?

_____
_____
_____

❖ In what ways can you deepen your relationship with Mary?

_____
_____
_____

Actions:

Pray the Rosary: This powerful prayer, which is centred on the life of Christ and the intercession of Mary, can help you draw closer to Jesus through the heart of His mother.

Reflect on the virtues of Mary: Consider how Mary's virtues, such as faith, humility, and obedience, can inspire and guide your spiritual journey.

Reach out to those in need: As Mary was a loving and compassionate mother, we can follow her example by showing care and compassion to those in need around us.

Learn about Marian apparitions: Studying the various apparitions of Mary throughout history can help deepen your understanding of her role in the Church and her ongoing presence in the lives of the faithful.

Consecrate yourself to Mary: Consider making a personal consecration to Jesus through Mary, entrusting your spiritual journey to her guidance and protection.

As we conclude Day 12, let us be grateful for the gift of Mary, our heavenly mother, and her powerful example of faith and obedience. May we learn from her life and follow her footsteps, trusting in God's plan for us and seeking her intercession as we continue our spiritual journey.

Tomorrow, we will explore another aspect of our spiritual life, but for now, let us take some time to reflect on our relationship with Mary and how we can grow closer to her. Remember how far you have come on this journey and know that each day brings new opportunities for growth and transformation.

As you go about your day, think about how you can be more like Mary, embodying her virtues and seeking her guidance. Through her intercession, may we draw closer to Jesus and continue to grow in our faith.

We invite you to join us again tomorrow as we delve deeper into our spiritual lives, further enriching our relationship with God and one another. Keep walking this Lenten journey with an open heart and may the grace of God be with you always.

Day 13: The Power of Silence

Dear friend, as we continue our journey through Lent, we come to a day where we focus on the power of silence.

In our fast-paced, noisy world, it is often difficult to find moments of quiet and stillness. Yet, it is in these moments of silence that we can deepen our relationship with God and truly listen to His voice in our hearts.

Throughout history, the great saints and mystics have extolled the virtues of silence. It is in the quiet that we can hear the gentle whisper of God, inviting us to draw closer to Him. In the Bible, we read about the prophet Elijah, who encountered God not in the powerful wind, earthquake, or fire, but in the still, small voice (1 Kings 19:11-13).

Silence is a precious gift, one that allows us to step away from the distractions and noise of the world and enter communion with our Creator. As we explore the importance of silence today, let us open our hearts to the transformative power that can be found in these moments of quiet reflection.

In our noisy world, silence is a rare and valuable commodity. It is in moments of stillness that we can truly listen to God's voice, allowing ourselves to be transformed by His presence in our lives. Silence provides us with an opportunity to connect with our inner selves and find peace amidst the chaos that often surrounds us.

As we seek to deepen our relationship with God during Lent, it is essential to cultivate moments of silence in our daily lives. These moments help us become more attuned to the presence of the Holy Spirit, guiding us on our spiritual journey. By stepping away from the distractions and noise of the world, we can create space for God to work in our hearts, shaping us into the people He calls us to be.

In the Gospels, we see Jesus often withdrawing to quiet places to pray (Luke 5:16). He sought solitude to commune with His Father and to be re-energised for His mission. As followers of Christ, we are called to follow His example and make time for silence in our own lives.

Questions:

- How does silence affect your spiritual life?

  _____

  _____

  _____

- How can you make space for silence in your daily routine?

  _____

  _____

  _____

Take a few moments to reflect on these questions and write down your thoughts in the space provided.

Action:

- Dedicate 20 minutes to silent meditation or contemplative prayer.

- Find a quiet space in your home or in nature where you can be alone and undisturbed. Create a comfortable and peaceful environment to help you focus on your time with God.

- Set a timer for 20 minutes and allow yourself to be fully present in the silence. Let go of any thoughts or distractions and simply be with God in the quiet.

- Try using a form of contemplative prayer, such as centring prayer or Lectio Divina, to guide your meditation. These practices can help you enter a deeper relationship with God through silence and listening.

- Consider incorporating moments of silence into your daily routine, such as during your morning or evening prayers or while commuting to work or school.

- ❖ Share your experiences of silence with a friend or family member, encouraging one another to make space for quiet reflection in your lives.

As we come to the end of our exploration of the power of silence, let us remember the importance of creating space for quiet reflection in our lives. It is in these moments that we can truly listen to the voice of God, deepening our relationship with Him and allowing ourselves to be transformed by His presence.

As you continue your Lenten journey, consider how you can intentionally cultivate moments of silence in your daily life. Perhaps you can begin or end each day with a few minutes of quiet reflection or find opportunities to step away from the noise and distractions of the world to be with God in stillness.

Remember the example of Jesus, who sought out solitude and silence to be with His Father. As you follow in His footsteps, may you find strength, peace, and guidance in the quiet moments with God.

As we look forward to tomorrow, let us be open to the ways God may be inviting us to grow and transform during this Lenten season. May our hearts be receptive to the grace and wisdom found in moments of silence, and may we be ever more attentive to the gentle whisper of God's voice in our lives.

Take a moment to reflect on how far you have come on this journey, and let that knowledge inspire you to continue forward with a renewed sense of purpose and commitment. May the peace and love of Christ be with you always as you continue to walk with Him through the remaining days of Lent and beyond.

Tomorrow, we will explore another aspect of our spiritual journey. Until then, let us hold one another in prayer and continue to seek the presence of God in the silence of our hearts.

Day 14: Building Community and Fellowship

As we journey through this Lenten season, I hope you have found new insights, spiritual growth, and moments of grace. Today, we will delve into the importance of community and fellowship, and how they play an essential role in our spiritual lives. Let us begin our reflection with St. Thomas Aquinas' Prayer for Charity.

Prayer:
Thomas Aquinas

Give me, O Lord,

a steadfast heart,

which no unworthy thought can drag downwards;

an unconquered heart,

which no tribulation can wear out;

an upright heart,

which no unworthy purpose may tempt aside.

Bestow upon me also,

O Lord my God,

understanding to know thee

diligence to seek thee,

wisdom to find thee,

and a faithfulness that may finally embrace thee;

through Jesus Chris our Lord.

Amen.

Reflection:

When Jesus walked the earth, He gathered a community around Him—His disciples, friends, and followers. They learned from Him, supported one another, and shared in the mission of spreading the Good News. This community was the foundation of the early Church, and it is through their fellowship that the message of Christ spread across the world.

Community and fellowship play an essential role in our spiritual lives. We are not meant to walk our faith journey alone but are called to support one another, share in our joys and sorrows, and grow together in faith. The community provides a space for us to be encouraged, challenged, and held accountable in our spiritual journey. It is within this sacred space that we can truly experience the love of Christ through the love of our brothers and sisters.

As members of the body of Christ, we have a responsibility to contribute to the spiritual growth of our community. This can be done by actively participating in church events, sharing our spiritual gifts, and being a source of encouragement and support for others. We are called to be the hands and feet of Christ, reaching out to those who are lost or struggling, and welcoming them into our community of faith.

Questions:

❖ How has your faith community influenced your spiritual journey?

By their warmth and kindness.
Support and prayer

❖ How can you contribute to your community's spiritual growth?

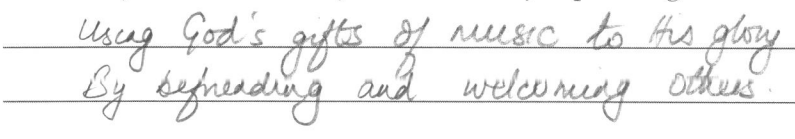

Using God's gifts of music to His glory
By befriending and welcoming others.

Take some time to reflect on these questions and write down your thoughts.

Action:

To help foster a sense of community and fellowship, consider participating in one or more of the following actions:

❖ Attend a church event or small group gathering to build fellowship.

❖ Volunteer for a ministry or outreach program in your parish.

❖ Offer to pray for or with someone in your community who needs support.

❖ Share your spiritual journey or testimony with others in your faith community.

❖ Invite a friend or neighbour to attend Mass or a church event with you.

Remember, these actions are merely suggestions. Feel free to adapt them to your unique situation or come up with your ideas for building community and fellowship.

As we conclude today's reflection, let us remember the importance of community and fellowship in our spiritual lives. We are not meant to walk this journey alone but are called to walk alongside our brothers and sisters in Christ. Let us continue to support and uplift one another, knowing that we are united in our love for Christ and our desire to grow in faith.

As we look forward to the next day, let us remain open to the ways God is calling us to deepen our relationships with our faith community. May we be inspired to reach out in love and support to those around us, sharing in the joys and challenges of our shared spiritual journey.

Take a moment to reflect on how far you have come on this journey, and let that knowledge inspire you to continue forward with a renewed sense of purpose and commitment. May the peace and love of Christ be with you always as you continue to walk in His footsteps.

In tomorrow's reflection, we will explore another important aspect of our spiritual lives. Let us remain open to the lessons and insights that God has in store for us, knowing that each day brings new opportunities for growth and deepening our relationship with Him.

As you go about your day, remember the power of community and the importance of fellowship in your spiritual journey. May you find inspiration in the examples of the early Church and the saints who had gone before us, as they, too, sought to build communities rooted in love, faith, and mutual support.

May God continue to bless and guide you as you journey through this Lenten season. Let us pray for one another and our faith communities that we may be strengthened and united in our mission to live out the Gospel message in our daily lives.

Amen.

Day 15: Encountering God in Nature

As we reach the halfway point of our Lenten journey together, I want to thank you for your commitment and perseverance. Each day, we have been exploring various aspects of our faith, deepening our understanding, and drawing closer to God. Today, we turn our attention to the beauty of God's creation and how we can encounter Him in nature.

In today's fast-paced and technology-driven society, it is all too easy to become disconnected from the natural world. We may spend our days indoors, working on computers or watching television, without even noticing the beauty that surrounds us. Yet, when we pause and take the time to truly observe and appreciate nature, we can discover God's presence in the most unexpected places.

In the words of the Psalmist, "The heavens declare the glory of God; the skies proclaim the work of his hands" (Psalm 19:1). From the vast expanse of the cosmos to the tiniest flower blooming in our backyard, God's handiwork is evident in all creation. In nature, we can find a glimpse of the divine, a reflection of the Creator's love and care for His creatures.

Reflection:

To cultivate a deeper appreciation for the natural world, we must first acknowledge our role as stewards of creation. God entrusted us with the responsibility of caring for the earth and all its creatures. We are called to be good stewards, not only for our own sake but also for the well-being of future generations.

Pope Francis, in his encyclical Laudato Si', highlights the importance of caring for our common home and the need for an ecological conversion. He writes, " Living our vocation to be protectors of God's handiwork is essential to a life of virtue; it is not an optional or a secondary aspect of our Christian experience " (Laudato Si', 217). In other words, caring for creation is an integral part of our spiritual journey and our call to holiness.

To encounter God in nature, we must first learn to be present and attentive. This requires us to slow down, step away from the distractions of our daily lives, and truly observe and appreciate the beauty that surrounds us. We can find God in the grandeur of a majestic mountain range, in the delicate petals of a blooming flower, or in the intricate patterns of a butterfly's wings. In each of these moments, we are reminded of God's love and care for His creation.

In addition to recognising God's presence in nature, we can also learn valuable spiritual lessons from the natural world. For example, the changing seasons can teach us about the cycles of life and the importance of trusting in God's plan. The persistence of a small plant pushing its way through a crack in the path can inspire us to persevere in our faith journey, even when faced with obstacles and challenges.

As we spend time in nature, we may also find that it provides an ideal setting for prayer and contemplation. The stillness and tranquillity of the outdoors can help us quieten our minds and open our hearts to the presence of God. Whether we are walking through a forest, sitting by a tranquil lake, or simply enjoying the view from our window, we can use these moments of solitude to connect with our Creator.

In addition to personal prayer and contemplation, nature can also provide a setting for communal worship and fellowship. Outdoor Masses, retreats, and prayer gatherings can help us experience God's presence in a new and profound way. By worshipping together in the beauty of creation, we can strengthen our bond with one another and deepen our connection to the divine.

Questions:

- How do you experience God in nature?

  In the vastness of the heavens

- How can you cultivate a deeper appreciation for the natural world?

  - By observation
  - Taking care of my tiny patch of nature.

- How can your encounters with nature strengthen your faith and spiritual growth?

  Gratitude and censelurity

- In what ways can you incorporate prayer and contemplation in nature into your daily routine?

- How can you participate in communal worship or fellowship that connects you with nature?

Take a moment to reflect on these questions and write your answers in the space provided.

Action:

5 suggestions informed by Catholic social teachings

- ❖ Make a conscious effort to spend time in nature each day, whether by taking a walk, gardening or simply enjoying a quiet moment outdoors. Use this time to pray, meditate, or simply appreciate the beauty of creation.

- ❖ Educate yourself about the importance of environmental stewardship and consider ways in which you can reduce your ecological footprint. This may include recycling, conserving water and energy, or supporting sustainable and ethical products.

- ❖ Participate in local environmental initiatives, such as tree planting, clean-up projects, or conservation efforts. By working together with others in your community, you can help protect and preserve the natural world for future generations.

- ❖ Advocate for environmental justice by raising awareness about the impact of pollution and climate change on marginalised communities and by supporting policies and initiatives that promote environmental sustainability and social equity.

- ❖ Organise or attend an outdoor prayer gathering or retreat, either individually or as part of your faith community. Use this opportunity to deepen your connection to God through the beauty of nature and the fellowship of others.

As we conclude today's journey of encountering God in nature, I hope that you feel inspired and motivated to explore the beauty of creation in new and meaningful ways. Remember that God's presence can be found in the most unexpected places and that by nurturing our connection to the natural world, we can deepen our relationship with the divine.

In the days and weeks ahead, I encourage you to embrace the opportunities that nature provides for prayer, contemplation, and spiritual growth. Whether you are marvelling at a magnificent sunset, listening to the soothing sounds of a babbling brook, or simply breathing in the fresh air, remember that these moments are a gift from God – an invitation to encounter Him in the beauty of creation.

As we continue our Lenten journey together, let us strive to be good stewards of the earth and to care for the world that God has so lovingly created. In doing so, we not only honour our Creator but also contribute to the well-being of all God's creatures.

May the wonder and beauty of nature bring you closer to God and enrich your spiritual journey. I look forward to walking with you in faith and fellowship as we explore new aspects of our faith in the days to come.

God bless you and your Lenten journey, my friend in Christ.

I am filled with gratitude for the opportunity to share this journey with you thus far. Your dedication to deepening your faith and relationship with God during this Lenten season is truly inspiring. Together, we have explored various aspects of our spiritual lives, and I hope that these experiences have brought us closer to God and each other.

As we move forward, let us continue to support and uplift one another, embracing the unique gifts and talents that each of us brings to our faith community. In doing so, we not only enrich our spiritual growth but also contribute to the building of God's kingdom here on earth.

As you continue to encounter God in nature, I encourage you to share your experiences and insights with others. By bearing witness to the beauty of creation and the presence of the divine in our lives, we can inspire and uplift those around us, helping them to see God's love and care in even the smallest details of the world.

In this spirit of sharing and fellowship, I invite you to join me tomorrow as we embark on a new aspect of our Lenten journey. Together, we will explore the importance of forgiveness and reconciliation, both in our personal lives and within our faith community. This is a vital aspect of our spiritual growth and an essential step towards deepening our relationship with God and one another.

As you go about your day, take a moment to pause and appreciate the beauty of creation around you. Remember that God is present in every leaf, every flower, and every blade of grass and that His love for us is as vast and infinite as the universe itself.

Let us go forward with joy and gratitude, trusting in God's abiding presence and love and carrying with us the lessons and experiences of our Lenten journey thus far. May the grace of God be with you today and always, my friend in Christ.

Day 16: Trusting in God's Providence

I am deeply grateful for the opportunity to walk alongside you on this Lenten journey, as we strive to deepen our faith and draw closer to God. Today, we delve into an essential aspect of our spiritual lives: trusting in God's providence. As we continue to navigate the challenges and uncertainties of life, our trust in God's plan for us serves as an anchor, steadying our hearts and minds and enabling us to move forward with confidence and hope.

Prayer:

St. Teresa of Avila

Let nothing disturb you,

Let nothing frighten you,

All things are passing away:

God never changes.

Patience obtains all things

Whoever has God lacks nothing;

God alone suffices.

St. Teresa of Avila's prayer, "Let Nothing Disturb You," serves as a powerful reminder of the importance of placing our trust in God's loving care and guidance. As we contemplate these beautiful words, let us open our hearts to the transformative power of faith and trust in God's providence.

Reflection:

The concept of God's providence is one that is both comforting and, at times, challenging to fully embrace. It requires us to relinquish control and surrender to the belief that God is always at work in our lives, even when the road ahead seems uncertain or fraught with difficulties.

Our journey through life is rarely smooth, and we often find ourselves faced with challenges that test our faith and trust in God. Yet, it is precisely in these moments that we are invited to lean into our faith and trust in God's plan for us, for it is only when we surrender our fears and anxieties to God that we can experience the true freedom and peace that comes from living in the knowledge of His abiding presence and love.

In our reflection, let us consider the ways in which trust in God's providence has shaped our spiritual lives. Perhaps there have been times when we have felt lost or overwhelmed, only to find ourselves guided and supported by God's grace. Or maybe there are areas of our lives where we still struggle to fully trust in God's plan, despite our desire to do so.

Whatever our experiences may be, let us take this opportunity to deepen our understanding of God's providence and its role in our spiritual growth. As we do so, we can begin to recognise the ways in which God is constantly at work in our lives, weaving together even the most seemingly insignificant events into a tapestry of grace and love.

Actions:

- ❖ Reflect on a time when you experienced God's providence in your life. Write about the circumstances and how they strengthened your trust in God.

- ❖ Identify an area of your life where you are struggling to trust in God's plan. Pray for the grace to surrender this worry or concern to God.

- ❖ Reach out to a friend or family member who may be struggling with trust in God's providence. Offer your support and prayers.

- ❖ Meditate on a Scripture passage that speaks to you about God's providence, such as Matthew 6:25-34 or Romans 8:28.

- ❖ Make a conscious effort to thank God each day for His providence, even in the smallest of ways.

I am truly grateful for the opportunity to share this journey with you, and I pray that our exploration of trust in God's providence has brought us closer to Him and one another. As we continue our Lenten path, let us remember that God's love and care for us are constant and unwavering, even in the face of life's uncertainties and challenges.

As we prepare to embark on the next stage of our journey, let us hold fast to the knowledge that we are never alone and that God's providence is always at work in our lives. May the grace of God continue to guide and strengthen us, both now and in the days to come.

With heartfelt gratitude and prayers for your journey, I invite you to join me tomorrow as we delve into the transformative power of gratitude and its role in our spiritual lives. Together, let us reflect on the countless ways in which we have been blessed and express our gratitude to God for His abundant gifts.

In closing, I would like to remind you of how far you have come on this journey thus far. Your dedication and openness to God's grace have undoubtedly touched the lives of others and deepened your faith. May you continue to be a shining light in our faith community, inspiring others through your trust in God's providence and your unwavering commitment to spiritual growth.

May God's love, peace, and joy surround you today and always. See you tomorrow, dear friend, as we take the next step on this beautiful journey together.

Day 17: The Practice of Discernment

As we journey together through these days of Lent, we find ourselves amid an ever-deepening relationship with our loving God. Today, we will explore the practice of discernment – a critical aspect of our spiritual lives which allows us to discover and follow God's will for us. By growing in our ability to discern, we can better align our hearts and minds with the desires of our Creator and experience the joy that comes from living in accordance with His plan.

Let us begin our reflection today by turning to St. Ignatius, who was renowned for his deep understanding and practice of discernment.

Prayer

Lord Jesus, teach me to be generous.

Teach me to serve as you deserve,

To give and not to count the cost,

To fight and not to heed the wounds,

To labor and not to seek to rest,

To give of my self and not ask for a reward,

Except the reward of knowing that I am doing your will.

St. Ignatius of Loyola, Pray for us.

Amen

Reflection:

Learning to Discern God's Will in Your Life

Discernment is the process of determining God's will in the various aspects of our lives. It involves prayerful consideration, self-examination, and seeking the guidance of the Holy Spirit to understand the path God has set before us. Discernment is a critical practice in our spiritual lives, as it allows us to make choices that are aligned with God's desires for us.

In discerning God's will, we must be attentive to the movements of the Holy Spirit within us. Often, God's will is revealed through the feelings of peace, joy, and consolation that accompany a particular decision or action. On the other hand, feelings of restlessness, agitation, or desolation may indicate that we are not following the path God has intended for us.

To improve our ability to discern God's will, we can engage in regular prayer and reflection, seeking the guidance of the Holy Spirit and asking for the grace to recognise God's presence in our lives. Additionally, we can consult with trusted spiritual advisors, such as priests, religious, or laypersons, who can offer valuable insights and support in our discernment process.

Questions:

- How do you currently practice discernment in your spiritual life?

- What are some ways you can improve your ability to discern God's will?

  By listening and having silence in my life.

- ❖ Can you recall a time when you felt a strong sense of God's guidance when making a decision? What was that experience like?

  _____
  _____
  _____

- ❖ How do you differentiate between your own desires and God's will for your life?

  _____
  _____
  _____

- ❖ How can you involve others in your discernment process, and what role can they play in helping you discern God's will?

  _____
  _____
  _____

Action:

Seeking God's Guidance through Prayer and Discernment

As we seek to grow in our practice of discernment, consider the following suggestions, informed by Catholic social teachings:

1. Set aside a specific time each day for prayer and reflection, asking the Holy Spirit to guide you in discerning God's will.
2. Engage in a spiritual retreat or day of recollection to deepen your relationship with God and focus on discernment.
3. Consult with trusted spiritual advisors who can offer valuable insights and support in your discernment process.

4. Pray with Scripture, allowing God's Word to speak to your heart and inform your discernment.
5. Practice the Ignatian Examen, a daily reflection exercise designed to help you recognise God's presence and discern His will in your everyday life.

In the space below, write down any thoughts or insights you have gained from today's reflection:

_____

_____

_____

_____

_____

As we conclude our time together today, let us remember that discernment is an ongoing process and an essential aspect of our spiritual lives. As we grow closer to God, we become more attuned to His voice and better equipped to discern His will in our daily lives.

Dear friend, as you continue this Lenten journey, I encourage you to remain open to the guidance of the Holy Spirit, trusting that God is ever-present and always seeking to draw you closer to Himself. May your heart be filled with the peace that comes from knowing and following God's will.

In the days ahead, continue to cultivate the practice of discernment, seeking God's guidance in all areas of your life. Remember that while discernment may sometimes be challenging, the Lord is always there to support and guide you. Trust in His loving providence and know that He is at work in your life, leading you ever closer to His heart.

Let us close our time together today by praying for the grace to trust in God's providence and the wisdom to discern His will:

St. Teresa of Avila's Let Nothing Disturb You

Let nothing disturb you,

Let nothing frighten you,

All things are passing away:

God never changes.

Patience obtains all things

Whoever has God lacks nothing;

God alone suffices.

Tomorrow, we will embark on another day of our Lenten journey, delving deeper into our faith and our relationship with God. May the Lord continue to bless and guide you, and may the peace of Christ be with you always.

Day 18: Cultivating a Servant's Heart

As we journey together through this season of Lent, today we will explore the importance of cultivating a servant's heart. This is a central aspect of our Christian faith, as Jesus Himself taught us that "the Son of Man did not come to be served, but to serve, and to give his life as a ransom for many" (Matthew 20:28). By developing a servant's heart, we follow Jesus' example, and our spiritual lives are enriched through selflessness and service.

In today's world, it can be challenging to focus on the needs of others, as we are often preoccupied with our own concerns and desires. Yet, as followers of Christ, we are called to prioritise the welfare of our neighbours and to give of ourselves in the service of others. In doing so, we draw closer to God and find true fulfilment in our lives.

Let us begin our reflection today by offering the beautiful prayer asking for the grace to serve with love.

Prayer:

O Lord, I desire to serve You with a love that is disinterested, not seeking any personal gain or reward, but purely desiring Your divine glory. May Your love be the motive of all my actions, so that I may be united with You in my service to others. Grant me the grace to forget myself, and to find my joy in giving and in sacrifice. Amen.

Reflection:

The Importance of Selflessness and Service in Our Spiritual Lives

As we reflect on the role of service in our spiritual lives, we can consider the numerous examples of selflessness that we find in the lives of the saints. These holy men and women devoted themselves to the needs of others, often at great personal cost. They understood that true happiness and spiritual growth are found not in accumulating possessions or seeking personal gain but in giving of oneself for the sake of others.

Jesus Himself demonstrated the ultimate act of service through His life, death, and resurrection. He washed the feet of His disciples, taught us to love our enemies, and ultimately laid down His life for our salvation. As we strive to follow in His footsteps, we must ask ourselves how we can develop a servant's heart in our own lives.

Questions:

❖ How does cultivating a servant's heart impact your relationship with God?

___

___

___

❖ In what ways do you currently serve others in your daily life?

By doing everything domestic for them at huge mental and emotional cost — I am an unpaid domestic servant, who is failing to hold back the tide of chaos.

❖ How can you more intentionally prioritise the needs of others over your own desires?

I cannot.

___

___

❖ What barriers or obstacles do you face in developing a servant's heart?

Exhaustion, resentment, anger, bitterness

___

❖ How can you learn from the example of Jesus and the saints in your journey towards selflessness and service?

_____

_____

_____

Take some time to reflect on these questions and write down your thoughts and insights.

Action:

Perform an Act of Service

Today, let us put our faith into action by performing an act of service for someone in our lives. This could be a friend, family member, or neighbour. Keep in mind that acts of service do not need to be grand gestures; even small acts of kindness can have a profound impact.

Some suggestions for acts of service include:

❖ Prepare a meal for a neighbour in need.

❖ Offer to run errands for an elderly or disabled person in your community.

❖ Volunteer your time at a local charity or non-profit organisation.

❖ Help a friend with a project or task they are struggling to complete.

❖ Offer a listening ear or a word of encouragement to someone who is going through a difficult time.

Remember that our acts of service should be guided by love and a genuine desire to help others. As we serve, let us seek to grow in humility and selflessness, remembering the words of Jesus: "Truly I tell you, whatever you did for one of the least of these brothers and sisters of mine, you did for me" (Matthew 25:40).

Dear friend, as we conclude our reflection on cultivating a servant's heart, let us be mindful of how we can put our faith into action in our everyday lives. By serving others with love and humility, we grow closer to God and deepen our spiritual lives.

As we look forward to tomorrow's journey, let us continue to seek God's grace and guidance in all that we do. May the Holy Spirit inspire us to live lives of selflessness and service, following the example of Jesus, our Lord and Saviour.

Take a moment now to thank God for the opportunity to serve others and to ask for His help in cultivating a servant's heart. Let us also pray for those in need of our love and assistance and for the strength to be a light in their lives.

May God bless you abundantly as you continue this Lenten journey, and may you find joy and fulfilment in serving others as Jesus has taught us. Remember how far you've come and look forward with anticipation to the spiritual growth that awaits you in the days ahead. Keep walking on this path, and know that the Lord is with you every step of the way.

In the name of the Father, and of the Son, and of the Holy Spirit. Amen.

Day 19: The Role of Suffering in Spiritual Growth

As we embark on Day 19 of our Lenten journey, we are invited to delve into a topic that touches each of our lives: suffering. It is a universal experience that can be difficult to understand and accept, but through our faith, we can find meaning and growth in our pain. Let us begin by praying St. Padre Pio's Prayer for Trust and Confidence, asking for the grace to see suffering as an opportunity for spiritual growth:

Prayer:

St. Padre Pio

O Lord, we ask for a boundless confidence and trust in Your divine mercy, and the courage to accept the crosses and sufferings which bring immense goodness to our souls and that of Your Church.

Help us to love You with a pure and contrite heart, and to humble ourselves beneath Your cross, as we climb the mountain of holiness, carrying our cross that leads to heavenly glory.

May we receive You with great faith and love in Holy Communion, and allow You to act in us, as You desire, for Your greater glory.

O Jesus, most adorable heart and eternal fountain of Divine Love, may our prayer find favor before the Divine Majesty of Your Heavenly Father.

Amen.

Reflection:

In the face of suffering, it is natural to ask, "why?" Why do we experience pain and hardship? Why does God allow suffering to occur? Throughout history, these questions have puzzled theologians, philosophers, and believers alike. While we may never fully comprehend the mystery of suffering, our faith can help us find meaning in our pain and use it as a catalyst for spiritual growth.

Suffering can serve many purposes in our spiritual lives. For one, it can be a powerful means of purification. As gold is refined in fire, so too are we purified through suffering. Our trials and tribulations can strip away the superficial aspects of our lives, leading us to a deeper, more authentic relationship with God. In this way, suffering can lead us to a greater appreciation of His love and mercy, as well as a heightened awareness of our dependence on Him.

Additionally, suffering can deepen our empathy and compassion for others. Amid our pain, we can better understand the struggles of those around us, allowing us to connect with them on a deeper level. This newfound compassion can inspire us to reach out and help others, furthering our spiritual growth and strengthening our connection to the greater human family.

Questions:

❖ How has suffering played a role in your spiritual journey?

_____

_____

_____

❖ Can you recall a time when suffering brought you closer to God? What did you learn from that experience?

❖ How can you find meaning and growth in suffering?

❖ How has suffering helped you develop empathy and compassion for others?

❖ In what ways can you help alleviate the suffering of those around you?
- Walking beside them in empathy, listening
- praying for them

Action:

Today, let us offer up a personal struggle or challenge in prayer, asking God to use it for our spiritual growth.

Consider the following suggestions informed by Catholic social teachings:

- ❖ Reflect on how your suffering has brought you closer to God and others and identify specific instances where you have grown through your pain.

- ❖ Pray for those who are suffering, especially those who may be experiencing similar trials as you.

- ❖ Reach out to someone you know who is struggling, offering a listening ear and a shoulder to lean on.

- ❖ Volunteer your time at a local charity or organisation that helps those who are suffering, such as a homeless shelter or a hospital.

- ❖ Educate yourself on the social issues that contribute to suffering in our world, and advocate for policies and initiatives that alleviate suffering and promote human dignity.

In conclusion, my dear friend, as we come to the end of Day 19 of our Lenten journey, let us remember that the journey of spiritual growth is not an easy one, and it requires constant effort and dedication. However, as you have seen throughout these daily reflections, there are many ways to deepen your relationship with God and strengthen your faith. By developing habits of prayer, embracing challenges with grace, practising generosity, and finding joy amid suffering, you can grow closer to God and become a more loving and compassionate person.

As you move forward on this journey, I encourage you to continue to seek out ways to strengthen your faith and deepen your spiritual life. Whether it's through daily prayer, attending church events, or volunteering in your community, there are countless ways to live out your faith and make a difference in the world.

Remember, the road ahead may not always be smooth, but with God by your side, you can overcome any obstacle and find true joy and fulfilment. I invite you to reflect on the journey you have taken so far and take some time to consider where you want to go from here. What habits can you continue to cultivate? What challenges do you want to embrace? How can you deepen your relationship with God and become the best version of yourself?

I wish you all the best on your journey and pray that you may continue to grow in faith and love. May God bless you always.

Day 20: The Beauty of God's Mercy

Welcome to Day 20 of our journey together, where we will reflect on the beauty of God's mercy. Have you ever experienced a moment in your life where you felt lost, alone, and in need of forgiveness? Perhaps you made a mistake that caused pain to others or yourself, and you thought that there was no way to make it right. But then, unexpectedly, you were shown mercy, love, and forgiveness that you didn't deserve but was given to you anyway.

God's mercy is just like that. It is love and forgiveness that are freely given to us, not because we deserve it, but because God loves us unconditionally. His mercy is so powerful that it can transform our lives, heal our wounds, and bring us back to a state of grace.

Prayer is an essential aspect of experiencing God's mercy. Today, we will pray the Divine Mercy Chaplet, a powerful prayer that focuses on God's mercy and its extension to others. This prayer reminds us that we are all sinners in need of God's mercy and that we should extend that same mercy to others.

As we reflect on the beauty of God's mercy, let us consider how we can be instruments of mercy to others. How can we show compassion and forgiveness to those who have wronged us, just as God has shown mercy to us?

Reflection:

Have you experienced God's mercy in your life? Take a moment to reflect on a time when you felt lost, alone, and in need of forgiveness. How did God's mercy help you at that moment? How has that experience impacted your life?

God's mercy is unconditional, and it is not limited to our past mistakes. It is available to us every day, and we can always turn to God for forgiveness and guidance. However, sometimes we struggle to accept God's mercy, or we might think that we do not deserve of it. But the truth is that God's mercy is a gift that we cannot earn or buy; it is freely given to us out of God's infinite love.

God's mercy is not just for ourselves; we are also called to extend that mercy to others. Sometimes, this might mean forgiving someone who has wronged us, even if they do not deserve it. Other times, it might mean showing compassion to someone who is struggling or in need of support. Whatever form it takes, extending God's mercy to others is an act of love and service that brings us closer to God.

Questions:

- ❖ How does the concept of God's mercy differ from human notions of justice and punishment?

  _____

  _____

  _____

- ❖ How can we overcome feelings of guilt or shame and accept God's mercy in our lives?

  _____

  _____

  _____

- ❖ In what ways can we extend God's mercy to others, even when it is difficult or uncomfortable?

  _____

  _____

  _____

- ❖ How can we balance the need for justice with the call to show mercy to others?

❖ What role does forgiveness play in experiencing and extending God's mercy?

Action:

Today's action is twofold: First, participate in the Sacrament of Reconciliation, also known as Confession. This sacrament is an opportunity to confess our sins, receive God's mercy and forgiveness, and commit ourselves to live a more virtuous life. Second, extend forgiveness to someone in your life who has wronged you, even if it is difficult.

Here are five suggestions for extending God's mercy to others, informed by Catholic social teachings:

❖ Volunteer at a local shelter or food bank to serve those in need.

❖ Donate to a charity that supports the marginalised or oppressed.

❖ Offer to help someone who is struggling with addiction or mental health issues.

❖ Advocate for policies that promote justice, fairness, and equality in your community and beyond.

❖ Participate in a dialogue or event that promotes understanding and compassion among different groups of people.

Remember, these are just suggestions, and you should choose an action that feels meaningful and appropriate for you. By taking action to extend God's mercy to others, we can deepen our own understanding of God's love and compassion.

Now, take some time to reflect on these questions and consider how you can take action to extend God's mercy to others in your life.

- ❖ What action will you take to extend God's mercy to others today?

  _____
  _____
  _____

- ❖ How will you prepare for the Sacrament of Reconciliation?

  _____
  _____
  _____

- ❖ What sins do you want to confess and seek forgiveness for?

  _____
  _____
  _____

- ❖ Whom do you need to forgive in your life, and how will you extend that forgiveness?

  _____
  _____
  _____

- ❖ How can you incorporate acts of mercy into your daily life going forward?

❖ What obstacles might you face in extending God's mercy to others, and how can you overcome them?

_____
_____
_____

As we close today's reflection, let us remember that God's mercy is a gift that we can never fully earn or repay. It is freely given to us, and we are called to extend that mercy to others in our lives. Through prayer, reflection, and action, may we deepen our understanding of God's love and mercy, and may we be instruments of that love to others.

May God's mercy be with you always.

Day 21: Nurturing Spiritual Friendships

Welcome to Day 21 of our spiritual journey. Today, we will be exploring the importance of nurturing spiritual friendships. As we progress on our spiritual journey, it is essential to have like-minded people who can support and encourage us. These are the individuals who will pray for us, hold us accountable, and help us grow in faith.

Having deep spiritual friendships is a blessing that cannot be quantified. The friendships we form on our spiritual journey are vital because they give us a sense of community and help us stay connected to God. These relationships are essential because they help us remain steadfast and committed to our faith.

When we have spiritual friendships, we can turn to our friends when we feel discouraged or overwhelmed. They can pray for us, encourage us, and remind us of God's promises. These relationships help us stay connected to our faith, even in difficult times.

It's essential to nurture these relationships because they are not easy to find. When we have a friend that shares our faith and values, it's essential to invest in that friendship. We need to make time for our friends, share our spiritual journeys with them, and pray for them.

we need to seek God's guidance in our relationships. We should pray for our friends and ask God to help us grow in our spiritual journeys together.

Reflection:

The Importance of Cultivating Deep, Spiritual Friendships

We are social beings, and we were created to have relationships. The relationships we have with people impact us, and this is why we need to be intentional about the friendships we cultivate. The Bible tells us in Proverbs 27:17, "Iron sharpens iron, and one man sharpens another."

This verse reminds us that we need to be in relationships that challenge us to grow and become better versions of ourselves. Spiritual friendships are relationships that help us grow in faith, wisdom, and knowledge.

When we have spiritual friends, we have people we can turn to when we need guidance and support. These are individuals who are not afraid to speak truthfully to us and help us stay grounded in our faith.

The importance of cultivating deep, spiritual friendships cannot be overemphasised.

These relationships are essential because they help us:

- Stay committed to our faith.
- Encourage us to grow spiritually.
- Provide a safe space to share our struggles and successes.
- Remind us of God's promises when we feel discouraged.
- Hold us accountable in our faith journey.

Questions:

- Who are the spiritual friends that have had a significant impact on your faith journey, and why?

    Fr Grant

- How do you maintain these relationships?

❖ What qualities do you look for in a spiritual friend?

_____

_____

_____

❖ How has having spiritual friendships helped you grow in your faith?

_____

_____

_____

❖ What steps can you take to cultivate deeper spiritual friendships?

_____

_____

_____

Action:

❖ Schedule a time to meet with a spiritual friend and share your faith journey with them.

❖ Pray for your spiritual friends and ask God to bless and guide your relationships.

❖ Join a small group or Bible study to meet new spiritual friends.

❖ Take the initiative to reach out to a friend you haven't spoken to in a while and reconnect.

❖ Commit to investing time in your spiritual friendships by regularly praying for and encouraging your friends.

❖ Now it's time for you to act. Take a moment to reflect on the questions above and choose one action step that you can implement today.

Congratulations on completing Day 21 of our spiritual journey. We hope that today's reflection has helped you understand the importance of cultivating deep, spiritual friendships.

As you continue your spiritual journey, we encourage you to seek out like-minded people who can support and encourage you. Invest time in these relationships, and pray for your friends, asking God to bless and guide your relationships.

Remember, spiritual friendships are essential for our growth as Christians, and we need to make an effort to nurture these relationships. Let us continue to seek God's guidance as we cultivate deep, meaningful relationships that will help us stay committed to our faith.

We invite you to join us tomorrow for Day 22, where we will be exploring the topic of gratitude. Let us continue this journey of spiritual growth together, seeking God's guidance and grace every step of the way.

Day 22: Recognising God's Love

Welcome to Day 22 of our journey towards recognising God's love. As we enter this new day, let us pause for a moment and reflect on where we have come from. In the past 21 days, we have explored various aspects of our spiritual life, delving deep into our faith and relationship with God. We have learned about forgiveness, trust, gratitude, and many other virtues that are essential to our growth as individuals and as children of God.

Today, we focus on recognising God's love, a love that is deep and unending. It is easy to get caught up in the busyness of life and forget to acknowledge the love that is constantly surrounding us. God's love is not just a feeling but a force that moves and guides us, giving us strength and courage to face the challenges of life.

As we begin this day, let us start with a prayer. Let us seek God as we ask for His guidance and love to fill our hearts.

Prayer:

O Lord my God, I pray that I may know you and love you more and more. I pray that I may see the signs of your love in my life and in the lives of those around me. Help me to recognise your presence in all things and to give thanks for your blessings. Fill me with your love, so that I may love others as you have loved me. Amen.

Reflection:

_____
_____
_____
_____
_____
_____

As we contemplate the depth of God's love, let us ask ourselves some questions to deepen our understanding and awareness of His love in our lives:

- How has God's love impacted your life, and how has it changed the way you view yourself and the world around you?

  I try to grasp how much God loves me as I am, even though I feel that I am not lovable much of the time.

- What are some of the ways you can cultivate a deeper relationship with God, and how can this help you experience His love more fully?

  To pray more, turn to Him, draw closer to Him

- In what ways can you show love and kindness to those around you, and how can you use your gifts and talents to serve others?

  With little acts of kindness

- How can you trust in God's love and plan for your life, even when things are difficult or uncertain?

  "Lord, I believe: help Thou my unbelief"

- How can you use your struggles and challenges as an opportunity to grow in your faith and deepen your understanding of God's love for you?

  Thinking of any similar things that our Lord experienced.
  Read the Bible more.

Now, let us move on to the action step for today. Here are some suggestions on how you can spend time in prayer, meditating on God's love, and allowing it to fill your heart:

Action:

- Spend time in nature, reflecting on the beauty of creation and the love that is woven throughout it.

- Read and meditate on Psalm 139, reflecting on the depth of God's knowledge and love for you.

- Write a letter to God, expressing your gratitude for His love and asking for His guidance in your life.

- Spend time in adoration before the Blessed Sacrament, allowing God's love to fill your heart.

- Take a moment to offer a kind word or gesture to someone in need, allowing God's love to flow through you and into the world.

Now, take a few moments to reflect on these actions and consider how you can incorporate them into your day-to-day life. Remember, these are suggestions, and you should feel free to modify them to fit your own spiritual practice and lifestyle.

As we come to the end of this day, let us reflect on the love that God has shown us and how we can share that love with others. Let us end with a prayer, asking God to guide us in our journey towards recognising His love and to fill us with His grace and peace.

Dear God, we thank you for the depth of your love, which surrounds us always. We ask that you guide us in our journey towards recognising and experiencing that love more fully. Fill us with your grace and peace so that we may share your love with others and be instruments of your peace in the world. Amen.

Thank you for joining me on this journey. I invite you to continue with us tomorrow as we delve deeper into the richness of God's love. Remember, each step we take brings us closer to a greater understanding of His love for us.

Day 23: The Power of the Eucharist

Welcome back to our journey of faith and spiritual growth. Today, we will be discussing the power of the Eucharist and its significance in our spiritual lives. As a Catholic, the Eucharist is central to our faith, and it is essential that we deepen our appreciation for it.

The Eucharist is the source and summit of our Christian life. It is the sacrament of the Body and Blood of Christ, which we receive during Mass. When we receive the Eucharist, we are united with Christ in a profound and intimate way. It is not just a symbol; it is the real presence of Christ in our lives.

St. Thomas Aquinas' Prayer for a Holy Communion reminds us of the importance of preparing ourselves before receiving the Eucharist. We should strive to be in a state of grace and free from mortal sin. We should also approach the altar with a sense of reverence and awe, knowing that we are receiving the body and blood of our Lord and Saviour.

Reflection:

How does the Eucharist nourish your faith? How can you prepare yourself to receive the Eucharist more fully?

The Eucharist is the bread of life that nourishes our souls. It is the source of our spiritual strength and sustenance. When we receive the Eucharist, we are strengthened in our faith and united with Christ. It helps us to grow in holiness and deepen our relationship with God.

To prepare ourselves to receive the Eucharist more fully, we must examine our conscience and confess our sins. We should also pray and meditate on the mystery of the Eucharist, remembering the sacrifice that Christ made for us on the cross. It is important to approach the altar with a heart full of gratitude and humility.

Questions:

- ❖ How has the Eucharist impacted your spiritual life?

- ❖ What steps can you take to deepen your appreciation for the Eucharist?

- ❖ How can you better prepare yourself to receive the Eucharist?

- ❖ What role does the Eucharist play in your daily life?

- ❖ How can you share the gift of the Eucharist with others?

Actions:

- ❖ Attend Mass and receive the Eucharist with a renewed sense of reverence.

- ❖ Spend time in Adoration, meditating on the mystery of the Eucharist.

- ❖ Make a conscious effort to live out the teachings of the Eucharist in your daily life, such as living a life of service to others.

- ❖ Share your love for the Eucharist with others, inviting them to attend Mass with you or sharing your own experience of the Eucharist.

- ❖ Support Catholic social teachings by volunteering at a local food bank or soup kitchen, advocating for social justice issues, or making a charitable donation to a Catholic organisation that helps those in need.

As we conclude our reflection on the power of the Eucharist, let us remember the words of St. John Paul II, who said, "The Eucharist is the secret of my day. It gives strength and meaning to all my activities of service to the Church and the world." Let us strive to deepen our appreciation for the Eucharist and make it the centre of our spiritual lives. Through our actions, let us live out the teachings of the Eucharist and share its gift with others.

As we move forward on our journey of faith, let us continue to reflect on our relationship with God and seek to deepen it each day. Tomorrow, we will be discussing the importance of prayer in our spiritual lives. May God bless you on your journey.

Day 24: The Call to Evangelisation

Welcome to Day 24 of our journey together. Today's theme is "The Call to Evangelisation". As we reflect on this theme, let us take a moment to ask for St. Francis Xavier's intercession through his prayer:

O God, who through the preaching of Saint Francis Xavier

won many peoples to yourself,

grant that the hearts of the faithful

may burn with the same zeal for the faith

and that Holy Church may everywhere rejoice

in an abundance of offspring.

Through our Lord Jesus Christ, your Son,

who lives and reigns with you in the unity of the Holy Spirit,

one God, for ever and ever.

Amen.

The call to evangelisation is not just for priests and religious, but for all baptised Christians. We are called to share the Good News with others and to spread the love of Christ wherever we go. However, this can be a daunting task, especially if we are unsure of how to go about it. That is why we turn to St. Francis Xavier,

Eternal God, Creator of all things, remember that You alone created the souls of unbelievers, which You have made according to Your Image and Likeness. Behold, O Lord, how to Your dishonour many of them are falling into Hell.Remember, O Lord, Your Son Jesus Christ, Who so generously shed His Blood and suffered for them. Do not permit that Your Son, Our Lord, remain unknown by unbelievers, but, with the help of Your Saints and the Church, the Bride of Your Son, remember Your mercy, forget their idolatry and infidelity, and make them know Him, Who You have sent, Jesus Christ, Your Son, Our Lord, Who is our salvation, our life, and our resurrection, through Whom we have been saved and redeemed, and to Whom is due glory forever. Amen.

Let us take a moment to reflect on how we can embrace our role in sharing the Good News with others. It can be as simple as sharing a spiritual insight or a personal testimony with someone in our lives. We can also be more intentional about our interactions with others, looking for opportunities to share the love of Christ in both words and actions.

Reflection:

As we reflect on our call to evangelisation, it is important to remember that this is not just a task we undertake but a way of life we are called to live. Evangelisation is not just about converting others but about sharing the love of Christ and building relationships with those around us.

One way we can live out our call to evangelisation is by being a witness to the Gospel in our everyday lives. This means being kind, compassionate, and loving towards others, even in the face of adversity. It means listening to others and being present to them, even when we may not agree with their beliefs or actions.

Another way we can share the Good News is by being intentional about our conversations with others. This may mean sharing a personal testimony or a spiritual insight or simply asking someone how they are doing and showing genuine interest in their lives.

As we embrace our call to evangelisation, it is important to remember that we are not alone. We have the support and guidance of the Holy Spirit and the example of countless saints who have gone before us. We can also turn to our community of faith for support and encouragement as we seek to share the love of Christ with others

Questions:

❖ What is your understanding of evangelisation?

❖ How has evangelisation impacted your own faith journey?

❖ What are some challenges you have faced in sharing the Good News with others?

❖ How can you be more intentional about your interactions with others to share the love of Christ?

❖ What can you do to support and encourage others in their call to evangelisation?

Actions:

Here are five suggestions informed by Catholic social teachings that can help us live out our call to evangelisation:

1. Build relationships with those who are marginalised: Jesus reached out to those who were on the fringes of society, and we are called to do the same. Take time to get to know people who are struggling, whether it's someone who is homeless, someone who is struggling with addiction, or someone who is lonely. Listen to their stories and show them that they are valued and loved.

2. Serve others: One of the most powerful ways we can share the love of Christ is by serving others. Find ways to volunteer in your community, whether it's at a local soup kitchen, a homeless shelter, or a nursing home. Look for opportunities to share your time and talents with others.

3. Practice hospitality: Invite others into your home and your life. Share meals together and create opportunities for conversation and connection. Show others the love of Christ through your generosity and hospitality.

4. Speak out against injustice: We are called to be voices for the voiceless and to work for justice and peace in the world. Look for ways to advocate for those who are marginalised and oppressed, whether it's through signing petitions, contacting your elected officials, or participating in peaceful protests.

5. Pray: Finally, remember that our call to evangelisation is rooted in prayer. Take time each day to pray for the people in your life who need to encounter the love of Christ. Ask the Holy Spirit to guide you and give you the courage and wisdom to share the Good News with others.

Write down some ways you can live out your call to evangelisation through these actions:

_____

_____

_____

_____

_____

_____

As we end our reflection on the call to evangelisation, let us remember that this is a journey we are on together. It is not something we do alone but something we do in the community with one another, supported by the Holy Spirit and the example of the saints who have gone before us.

Let us continue to embrace our call to evangelisation, not as a task to be completed but as a way of life to be lived. Let us be witnesses to the love of Christ in our everyday interactions with others, and let us be intentional about building relationships with those around us.

May the intercession of St. Francis Xavier and the guidance of the Holy Spirit inspire us to share the Good News with others and to bring the light of Christ into the world.

Day 25: Practicing Gratitude in All Circumstances

As we continue our journey of spiritual growth, we have reached Day 25. You have shown immense dedication and perseverance in your quest to strengthen your relationship with God. Today, we will be focusing on the practice of gratitude in all circumstances, regardless of how challenging they may be. I am honoured to walk with you on this path and share in your spiritual discoveries.

Gratitude is a powerful emotion that can transform our perspective on life and help us to recognise the countless blessings that God has bestowed upon us. It is an essential part of our spiritual development, as it allows us to appreciate the beauty and wonder of the world, even amid suffering and adversity. As St. Ignatius of Loyola once said, "In all things, give thanks." In today's chapter, we will explore the importance of practising gratitude in all circumstances and how it can profoundly impact our spiritual life.

Reflection:

In life, we will inevitably face challenges and hardships. These difficult moments can leave us feeling overwhelmed, disheartened, and questioning God's presence in our lives. However, it is precisely in these times that we must strive to maintain a grateful heart, as it allows us to see beyond our immediate circumstances and recognise the bigger picture of God's love and grace.

When we practice gratitude, we shift our focus from what is lacking in our lives to the abundance of blessings that surround us. This shift in perspective can have a profound impact on our spiritual well-being, as it reminds us that God's love is ever-present and unwavering, even in the most trying times. Furthermore, by acknowledging the good in our lives, we open ourselves up to receiving even more blessings and opportunities for growth.

In difficult circumstances, cultivating gratitude may seem like an insurmountable task. However, with intentional effort and prayer, we can train our minds to see the good in every situation. One powerful way to do this is through the practice of St. Ignatius' Prayer of Gratitude. This prayer encourages us to reflect on our day and identify moments where we experienced God's presence, love, and grace. By doing so, we begin to see how God is always at work in our lives, even when we may not feel it.

Questions:

- ❖ How has practising gratitude in your daily life impacted your relationship with God?

  _____
  _____
  _____

- ❖ In what ways can you remind yourself to cultivate gratitude, even during difficult times?

  _____
  _____
  _____

- ❖ How can you use your gratitude practice to deepen your faith and trust in God's plan for your life?

  _____
  _____
  _____

- ❖ Can you recall a challenging situation where you found reasons to be grateful? How did it change your perspective on the situation?

  _____
  _____
  _____

❖ How can you share the gift of gratitude with others and help them see the blessings in their own lives?

_____

_____

_____

Actions:

As we strive to practice gratitude in all circumstances, consider the following five suggestions informed by Catholic social teachings.

Remember, these are not prescriptive but rather meant to inspire and guide your own personal journey.

❖ Reflect on the inherent dignity of every person. Recognise the unique gifts and talents that everyone brings to the world and thank God for the opportunity to encounter them.

❖ Consider how you can practice solidarity with those who are less fortunate or marginalised. Express gratitude for the ability to support and uplift others through acts of kindness and compassion.

❖ Contemplate the beauty and wonder of God's creation. Thank God for the natural world and the ways it nourishes and sustains us.

❖ Acknowledge the importance of family and community in your life. Give thanks for love and support you receive from those around you and consider how you can strengthen these relationships.

❖ Reflect on your own gifts and abilities. Thank God for the ways you have been uniquely created, and consider how you can use your talents to serve others and glorify God.

In the space provided below, write your answers and reflections on these suggestions. Remember, this is a personal journey, and your responses will help you grow and deepen your gratitude practice.

_____
_____
_____
_____
_____
_____

As we conclude Day 25, I hope that you have found inspiration and encouragement in the practice of gratitude. It is truly a transformative force that can deepen our relationship with God and help us navigate the complexities of life with grace and hope. As you continue this spiritual journey, remember to maintain a grateful heart in all circumstances and trust in God's unwavering love for you.

As we look forward to Day 26, let us rejoice in how far we have come and anticipate the growth and discoveries that lie ahead. Together, we will continue to explore the richness of our faith and our relationship with God, drawing ever closer to the divine presence that guides and sustains us.

May you be blessed with a heart full of gratitude and a spirit of resilience as we continue this journey together.

Day 26: Embracing the Beatitudes

Welcome, dear reader, to Day 26 of our spiritual journey. Your dedication and commitment to deepening your relationship with God are truly inspiring, and I am honoured to accompany you on this path. Today, we will be embracing the Beatitudes, a set of teachings from Jesus that provide a blueprint for living a blessed and spiritually fulfilling life.

The Beatitudes, found in Matthew 5:3-12, are part of Jesus' Sermon on the Mount and offer a powerful reminder of the values and attitudes that we should strive to embody in our daily lives. As we reflect on these teachings, we will explore how we can better understand and live out the Beatitudes, drawing closer to the heart of God.

Reflection:

The Beatitudes are not only a collection of sayings but a guide for our spiritual journey. Each Beatitude offers a unique perspective on the qualities and virtues that we should strive to develop within ourselves. By embracing the wisdom of the Beatitudes, we can cultivate a life that is rich in love, compassion, and humility.

To understand and live out the Beatitudes in our daily lives, we must first recognise that they are not merely external actions but rather internal transformations. Each Beatitude calls us to examine our hearts and minds, challenging us to grow and evolve in our relationship with God and others. This growth is a lifelong process, one that requires patience, persistence, and prayer.

As we delve deeper into the teachings of the Beatitudes, we can begin to see how they are interconnected and build upon one another. For example, when we embrace poverty of spirit, we recognise our dependence on God and our need for His grace. This humility enables us to mourn the brokenness of the world and ourselves, leading to a deep and abiding sense of compassion. As we continue this path, we become meek and hunger for righteousness, embracing the peace-making and merciful nature of God's love.

Questions:

- Which of the Beatitudes resonates with you the most, and why?

- How have you experienced the blessings promised in the Beatitudes in your own life?

- How can the Beatitudes help you to deepen your relationship with God and others?

- What challenges might you face when trying to live out the Beatitudes in your daily life?

- Can you identify a specific area in your life where you can better embody the teachings of the Beatitudes?

Actions:

As you continue to reflect on the Beatitudes and their impact on your spiritual life, consider the following five suggestions informed by Catholic social teachings.

These suggestions are not prescriptive but are intended to guide and inspire you in your journey.

- ❖ Choose one Beatitude to focus on and practice it throughout the day. As you do so, consider how you can embody the spirit of the Beatitude in your thoughts, words, and actions.

- ❖ Reflect on how the Beatitudes call us to promote the common good and work for the well-being of all people. Consider specific ways that you can put this into practice in your community.

- ❖ Meditate on the concept of human dignity, as emphasised in the Beatitudes. Think about how you can recognise and honour the dignity of others in your daily interactions.

- ❖ Contemplate the importance of solidarity and unity in the Beatitudes. Consider how you can promote a spirit of unity and collaboration in your family, workplace, and community.

- ❖ Pray for the grace and strength to live out the teachings of the Beatitudes in your life. Ask God to guide you and help you grow in holiness and virtue.

In the space provided below, write your answers and reflections on these suggestions. Remember, this is a personal journey, and your responses will help you grow and deepen your understanding of the Beatitudes.

_____
_____
_____
_____

As we conclude Day 26, I hope you have found inspiration and encouragement in embracing the teachings of the Beatitudes. By striving to live out these virtues in our daily lives, we can grow closer to God and experience the profound blessings that Jesus promised.

As we look forward to Day 27, let us rejoice in the progress we have made on this spiritual journey and eagerly anticipate the continued growth and discoveries that await us. Together, we will delve deeper into the mysteries of our faith and strengthen our relationship with God, guided by the wisdom and teachings of Jesus Christ.

May the Beatitudes serve as a beacon of light on your path, illuminating the way to a life of love, compassion, and holiness. And may you be abundantly blessed as you continue this journey with a heart open to the transformative power of God's grace.

Day 27: The Gift of Hope

As we embark on Day 27 of our spiritual journey together, I want to express my gratitude for your dedication and commitment to this transformative process. It is truly an honour to walk alongside you as we explore the depths of our faith and nurture our relationship with God. Today, we will focus on the gift of hope, a vital element in our spiritual lives that sustains us through both joy and adversity.

Hope is a powerful and essential force in our spiritual journey, helping us to remain steadfast in our faith despite the challenges we face. Through the grace of hope, we can persevere with trust in God's love and plan for our lives. In today's chapter, we will delve into the importance of hope and explore how we can cultivate and nurture this vital virtue in our daily lives.

Reflection:

Hope is often described as the anchor of the soul, grounding us in our faith and trust in God's goodness. It is a gift from God that enables us to see beyond the trials and tribulations of this world and look forward to the eternal happiness and peace promised by Christ. In times of doubt, fear, or suffering, hope can provide us with the strength and courage to continue our spiritual journey.

Cultivating hope in our spiritual lives requires an intentional effort to nurture our relationship with God through prayer, reflection, and the sacraments. By deepening our connection to the divine, we strengthen our trust in God's promises and develop a more profound sense of hope. Moreover, as we grow in hope, we become better equipped to share this gift with others and offer them the encouragement and support they need to face life's challenges.

In our daily lives, we can cultivate hope by focusing on the presence of God in every moment, recognising the countless ways He blesses and sustains us. We can also practice gratitude for the good things in our lives, even amid difficulties, as this helps us to maintain a hopeful perspective. Furthermore, by seeking the guidance and wisdom of the Holy Spirit in our decisions and actions, we can foster a spirit of hope that permeates every aspect of our lives.

Questions:

- ❖ How does hope sustain you in your spiritual journey?

  _____

  _____

  _____

- ❖ In what areas of your life do you need to cultivate hope?

  _____

  _____

  _____

- ❖ How can you nurture hope in your relationship with God and others?

  _____

  _____

  _____

- ❖ How can you share the gift of hope with those around you who may be struggling?

  _____

  _____

  _____

❖ In what ways has your hope in God's promises been tested or strengthened throughout your life?

_____

_____

_____

Actions:

As you continue to reflect on the gift of hope, consider the following five suggestions informed by Catholic social teachings.

These suggestions are not prescriptive but are intended to guide and inspire you in your journey.

❖ Pray for someone who is struggling, asking God to fill them with hope and peace. Offer words of encouragement and support to let them know they are not alone in their journey.

❖ Reflect on the importance of hope in promoting the common good and working for justice in society. Consider specific ways you can advocate for and support the needs of the most vulnerable in your community.

❖ Meditate on the concept of human dignity and how hope is essential to recognising and honouring the inherent worth of every person. Think about how you can promote hope by treating others with kindness and respect.

❖ Contemplate the power of community and solidarity in nurturing hope. Consider how you can foster hope within your family, workplace, and community by promoting a spirit of unity and collaboration.

❖ Pray for the grace to remain steadfast in hope, trusting in God's love and plan for your life. Ask for the strength to persevere in your spiritual journey, even in times of doubt or difficulty.

In the space provided below, write your answers and reflections on these suggestions. Remember, this is a personal journey, and your responses will help you grow and deepen your understanding of the gift of hope.

_____
_____
_____
_____
_____
_____

As we conclude Day 27, I hope that you have been inspired and encouraged by the gift of hope in your spiritual journey. By cultivating and nurturing hope in our daily lives, we can draw closer to God and experience the peace and joy that come from trusting in His love and promises.

As we eagerly anticipate Day 28, let us rejoice in the progress we have made on this spiritual journey and look forward to the continued growth and discoveries that await us. Together, we will explore the riches of our faith and deepen our relationship with God, guided by His grace and the wisdom of the Holy Spirit.

May hope be a guiding light on your path, illuminating the way to a life of faith, trust, and love. And may you be abundantly blessed as you continue this journey with an open heart filled with the transformative power of God's grace.

Day 28: The Example of the Saints

As we embark on Day 28 of our spiritual journey, I am filled with gratitude for your dedication and commitment to deepening your relationship with God. Your presence on this path is truly a blessing, and I am honoured to accompany you as we explore the richness of our faith. Today, we will turn our attention to the example of the saints, whose lives of holiness and devotion offer us inspiration and guidance on our own spiritual journey.

The saints are men and women who have gone before us, living lives of extraordinary faith, courage, and love for God. By studying their lives and teachings, we can learn valuable lessons about the pursuit of holiness and the transformative power of God's grace. In today's chapter, we will delve into the lives of the saints and explore how their examples can inform and inspire our spiritual journey.

Reflection:

The saints come from a wide variety of backgrounds and circumstances, yet they all share a common goal: the pursuit of holiness and union with God. By learning from their experiences, we can glean insights into how to deepen our own spiritual lives and draw closer to the heart of God.

One of the most important lessons we can learn from the saints is the importance of humility and self-surrender to the will of God. The saints recognised their weaknesses and limitations, relying on God's grace to transform them and empower them to live lives of virtue and holiness. By embracing a spirit of humility and dependence on God, we can open our hearts to the transformative power of His grace.

Another key lesson from the lives of the saints is the power of prayer and contemplation. The saints were deeply committed to nurturing their relationship with God through prayer, meditation, and the study of Scripture. By following their example and making prayer a central part of our daily lives, we can strengthen our connection to the divine and experience the peace and joy that come from a life rooted in God's love.

Questions:

- Which saint's life inspires you the most, and why?

- How can the example of the saints guide your spiritual journey?

- What lessons can you learn from the lives of the saints about the pursuit of holiness?

- How can the saints' devotion to prayer and contemplation inspire your spiritual practices?

- In what ways can you strive to emulate the virtues and qualities of the saints in your daily life?

Actions:

As you continue to reflect on the example of the saints and their impact on your spiritual life, consider the following five suggestions informed by Catholic social teachings.

These suggestions are not prescriptive but are intended to guide and inspire you in your journey.

- ❖ Read a biography or writings of a saint who inspires you. As you do so, consider how their life and teachings can inform and guide your spiritual journey.

- ❖ Reflect on the importance of the saints in promoting the common good and working for justice in society. Consider specific ways you can follow their example in advocating for and supporting the needs of the most vulnerable in your community.

- ❖ Meditate on the concept of human dignity and how the saints honoured the inherent worth of every person through their lives of charity and service. Think about how you can follow their example by treating others with kindness and respect.

- ❖ Contemplate the power of community and solidarity in the lives of the saints. Consider how you can foster a spirit of unity and collaboration within your family, workplace, and community, following the example of the saints.

- ❖ Pray for the intercession of the saints, asking them to guide and protect you on your spiritual journey. Seek their wisdom and inspiration as you strive to grow in holiness and virtue.

In the space provided below, write your answers and reflections on these suggestions. Remember, this is a personal journey, and your responses will help you grow and deepen your understanding of the lives of the saints and their impact on your spiritual life.

_____
_____
_____
_____
_____
_____

As we conclude Day 28, I hope that you have been inspired and encouraged by the example of the saints and their pursuit of holiness. By studying their lives and teachings, we can learn valuable lessons that will help us grow in our spiritual journey and draw closer to the heart of God.

As we eagerly anticipate Day 29, let us rejoice in the progress we have made on this spiritual journey and look forward to the continued growth and discoveries that await us. Together, we will explore the riches of our faith and deepen our relationship with God, guided by His grace and the wisdom of the Holy Spirit.

May the example of the saints inspire and challenge you as you continue your path towards holiness and union with God. And may you be abundantly blessed as you continue this journey with an open heart filled with the transformative power of God's grace.

Day 29: Living a Life of Simplicity

As we embark on Day 29 of our spiritual journey together, I am filled with admiration for your commitment to deepening your relationship with God. It has been an honour to accompany you on this path, and I am grateful for the opportunity to share in your journey of faith. Today, we will explore the importance of simplicity and detachment from material possessions in our spiritual lives, drawing inspiration from the teachings of St. Francis of Assisi and the wisdom of Catholic social teachings.

In a world that often values material wealth and accumulation, the practice of simplicity can help us refocus our attention on what truly matters: our relationship with God and our commitment to serving others. By embracing a life of simplicity, we can create space for spiritual growth and foster a deeper connection to the divine.

Reflection:

The pursuit of simplicity in our lives is not merely about decluttering or minimising material possessions but rather about cultivating an attitude of detachment and a spirit of gratitude for the gifts we have been given. By practising simplicity, we acknowledge that everything we have is a gift from God and that our true security and fulfilment come not from material possessions but from our relationship with Him.

One of the ways in which we can practise simplicity in our daily lives is by examining our attachment to material possessions and considering how these attachments might be hindering our spiritual growth. This process can involve both internal reflection and practical action, such as decluttering our homes or donating unneeded items to those in need.

Another important aspect of simplicity is the recognition of the interconnectedness of all creation and our responsibility to care for the earth and its resources. By embracing simplicity, we can live more sustainably and equitably, ensuring that the needs of all people and the planet are met.

Questions:

- How does simplicity contribute to your spiritual growth?

- In what ways can you practice simplicity in your daily life?

- How can the teachings of St. Francis of Assisi on simplicity and detachment inspire your spiritual journey?

- How can living a life of simplicity help you better serve others and care for the earth?

- What practical steps can you take to simplify your life and foster a spirit of detachment from material possessions?

Actions:

As you continue to reflect on the importance of simplicity and detachment in your spiritual life, consider the following five suggestions informed by Catholic social teachings.

These suggestions are not prescriptive but are intended to guide and inspire you in your journey.

- ❖ Declutter your living space, focusing on items that you no longer need or use. Donate these items to a local charity, helping those in need and fostering a spirit of detachment from material possessions.

- ❖ Reflect on your consumption habits and consider ways in which you can live more simply and sustainably, such as reducing waste, conserving energy, and supporting local and ethically produced goods.

- ❖ Spend time in nature, cultivating a spirit of gratitude and awe for the beauty of creation. Use this time to reflect on your responsibility to care for the earth and all its creatures.

- ❖ Engage in acts of service, volunteering your time and resources to support those in need in your community. By focusing on the needs of others, you can deepen your sense of detachment from material possessions.

- ❖ Meditate on the teachings of St. Francis of Assisi and other saints who embraced a life of simplicity and detachment. Draw inspiration from their example as you seek to deepen your own spiritual life.

In the space provided below, write your answers and reflections on these suggestions. Remember, this is a personal journey, and your responses will help you grow and deepen your understanding of the importance of simplicity and detachment in your spiritual life.

_____

_____

_____

_____

_____

_____

As we conclude Day 29, I hope that you have found inspiration and encouragement in the pursuit of simplicity and detachment from material possessions. Embracing a life of simplicity can help us refocus our attention on our relationship with God and our commitment to serving others, fostering spiritual growth and a deeper connection to the divine.

As we eagerly anticipate Day 30, let us rejoice in the progress we have made on this spiritual journey and look forward to the continued growth and discoveries that await us. Together, we will explore the riches of our faith and deepen our relationship with God, guided by His grace and the wisdom of the Holy Spirit.

May the practice of simplicity and detachment enrich your spiritual life and draw you ever closer to the heart of God. And may you be abundantly blessed as you continue this journey with an open heart filled with the transformative power of God's grace.

Day 30: Cultivating the Virtue of Temperance

Dear reader, congratulations on reaching Day 30 of our spiritual journey together! Your dedication to deepening your relationship with God is truly inspiring, and I am grateful for the opportunity to accompany you on this path. As we continue to explore various aspects of our faith, today we will focus on cultivating the virtue of temperance. This virtue encourages self-control and balance in all aspects of our lives, allowing us to grow in holiness and draw closer to God.

In our modern world, it can be challenging to maintain balance and self-control amidst the numerous distractions and temptations that surround us. However, the virtue of temperance offers a valuable guide for navigating these challenges and staying grounded in our faith.

Reflection:

Temperance is a virtue that helps us regulate our desires and appetites, ensuring that we maintain a healthy balance in our lives. It encourages self-control and moderation in all aspects of our lives, including our thoughts, words, and actions. By practising temperance, we learn to resist the pull of excess and cultivate an inner peace that allows us to be more attuned to the voice of God.

Developing the virtue of temperance can support our spiritual growth in several ways. Firstly, it helps us to maintain a clear and focused mind, free from distractions that can hinder our relationship with God. Secondly, temperance fosters humility and self-awareness, allowing us to recognise our limitations and depend more fully on God's grace.

Cultivating temperance in our lives may involve identifying areas where we struggle with self-control or balance and then taking intentional steps to address these challenges. This process can be aided by prayer, reflection, and the support of a spiritual director or trusted friend.

Questions:

- How does temperance support your spiritual growth?

　

- What areas of your life need more balance and self-control?

　

- How can the practice of temperance help you to resist temptations and distractions in your daily life?

　

- What role does humility play in the cultivation of temperance?

　

- How can you seek support from others as you work to develop the virtue of temperance?

Actions:

As you continue to reflect on the importance of temperance in your spiritual life, consider the following five suggestions informed by Catholic social teachings.

These suggestions are not prescriptive but are intended to guide and inspire you in your journey.

- ❖ Identify one area where you struggle with self-control and make a conscious effort to practice temperance. This may involve setting boundaries, seeking accountability, or developing a regular prayer routine to help you stay focused.

- ❖ Reflect on your daily habits and routines, considering how they contribute to or detract from a balanced and temperate lifestyle. Make any necessary adjustments to support your spiritual growth and well-being.

- ❖ Seek out the wisdom and guidance of a spiritual director or trusted friend who can support you in your journey toward greater self-control and balance.

- ❖ Engage in regular prayer and meditation, asking God for the grace to grow in temperance and to resist the temptations that may arise in your daily life.

- ❖ Study the lives of the saints who exemplified the virtue of temperance, drawing inspiration from their example and seeking their intercession as you strive to cultivate this virtue in your own life.

In the space provided below, write your answers and reflections on these suggestions. Remember, this is a personal journey, and your responses will help you grow and deepen your understanding of the importance of temperance in your spiritual life.

_____
_____
_____
_____
_____
_____

As we conclude Day 30, I hope that you have found inspiration and encouragement in the pursuit of temperance and self-control. Cultivating this virtue can have a profound impact on our spiritual lives, helping us to maintain balance, resist temptation, and draw closer to God.

As we continue our spiritual journey together, let us celebrate the progress we have made and eagerly anticipate the days ahead. Each day offers new opportunities for growth, discovery, and a deeper connection to the divine. Let us continue to walk this path with open hearts, seeking the guidance and wisdom of the Holy Spirit along the way.

May the practice of temperance bring you a greater sense of peace and balance in your life, as well as a deeper awareness of God's presence in your daily experiences. May your journey be blessed, and may you continue to grow in holiness and love as you strive to follow the path that God has laid before you.

Day 31: The Spiritual Works of Mercy

Dear reader, congratulations on reaching Day 31 of our spiritual journey together! Your commitment and desire to grow in faith are truly inspiring. As we continue to delve deeper into various aspects of our faith, today we will focus on the Spiritual Works of Mercy. These works are an integral part of our Catholic tradition, inviting us to reach out to others with compassion and love, both spiritually and emotionally.

As we explore the Spiritual Works of Mercy, we will reflect on their importance in our daily lives and consider ways to incorporate them into our spiritual practice. By doing so, we can enrich our relationship with God and deepen our commitment to living out our faith in service to others.

Reflection:

The Spiritual Works of Mercy are a set of seven practices that guide us in offering spiritual and emotional support to others. They include instructing the ignorant, counselling the doubtful, admonishing the sinner, bearing wrongs patiently, forgiving offences willingly, comforting the afflicted, and praying for the living and the dead.

These works remind us of our responsibility to care for the spiritual well-being of others and to share in their burdens and struggles. By practising the Spiritual Works of Mercy, we not only extend God's love and compassion to those in need, but we also grow in our own faith and deepen our relationship with God.

Each Spiritual Work of Mercy offers unique opportunities to serve others and to grow in holiness. For example, instructing the ignorant may involve sharing our faith with those who have not yet encountered Christ, while counselling the doubtful might require offering guidance and support to someone struggling with their faith.

As we reflect on these works, it is important to consider which resonates most deeply with us and to seek opportunities to incorporate them into our daily lives. By doing so, we can truly live out our faith in service to others and grow in our relationship with God.

Questions:

❖ Which Spiritual Work of Mercy resonates with you the most, and why?

_____
_____
_____

❖ How can you incorporate these works into your daily life?

_____
_____
_____

❖ In what ways have you already practised the Spiritual Works of Mercy?

_____
_____
_____

❖ How have the Spiritual Works of Mercy enriched your relationship with God and others?

_____
_____
_____

❖ What challenges might you face as you seek to practice the Spiritual Works of Mercy, and how can you overcome them?

_____
_____
_____

Actions:

As you reflect on the Spiritual Works of Mercy and their importance in your spiritual life, consider the following five suggestions informed by Catholic social teachings.

These suggestions are intended to guide and inspire you in your journey, rather than prescribe a specific course of action.

- ❖ Choose one Spiritual Work of Mercy to practice today. Be intentional in seeking opportunities to serve others and share God's love and compassion with them.

- ❖ Reflect on past experiences where you have practised the Spiritual Works of Mercy. What lessons have you learned from these experiences, and how can you apply them to your future practice of these works?

- ❖ Engage in regular prayer and meditation, asking God for the grace and guidance to grow in your practice of the Spiritual Works of Mercy.

- ❖ Seek out a spiritual mentor or a trusted friend who can support you in your journey to incorporate the Spiritual Works of Mercy into your daily life.

- ❖ Study the lives of saints who exemplified the Spiritual Works of Mercy, drawing inspiration from their example and seeking their intercession as you strive to live out these works in your own life.

In the space provided below, write your answers and reflections on these suggestions. Remember, this is a personal journey, and your responses will help you grow and deepen your understanding of the importance of the Spiritual Works of Mercy in your spiritual life.

_____
_____
_____

As we conclude Day 31 of our journey together, let us celebrate the progress we have made and the growth we have experienced in our spiritual lives. The Spiritual Works of Mercy offer us a beautiful opportunity to deepen our relationship with God and to serve others with compassion and love.

As you continue to explore and practice the Spiritual Works of Mercy, may your heart be filled with the joy and peace that come from embracing God's call to love and serve one another. Each day offers new opportunities for growth and discovery, and as you strive to live out your faith through these works, you will undoubtedly draw closer to God and experience His abundant grace.

May your journey be blessed and fruitful, and may you continue to grow in holiness and love as you embrace the Spiritual Works of Mercy in your daily life. Tomorrow, we will embark on another day of spiritual exploration and growth, and I eagerly look forward to sharing that journey with you.

Day 32: The Importance of Spiritual Reading

Welcome, dear reader, to Day 32 of our shared spiritual journey. Your dedication and desire for growth in faith are truly inspiring. As we continue to explore various aspects of our faith, today, we will focus on the importance of spiritual reading. Reading spiritually enriching material is an essential practice for nurturing and deepening our faith.

Spiritual reading can take many forms, from Scripture to the writings of saints, Church Fathers, and contemporary authors. By engaging with these texts, we can gain new insights into our faith, be inspired by the examples of others, and draw closer to God. Let us delve into the role of spiritual reading in our lives and consider how we can incorporate this practice into our daily routine.

Reflection:

Spiritual reading is a time-honoured practice that has played a crucial role in the spiritual lives of countless individuals throughout history. By engaging with religious texts and the writings of others who have sought to deepen their faith, we can open our hearts and minds to the wisdom and guidance that these works have to offer.

The role of spiritual reading in nurturing our faith cannot be overstated. Through engaging with these texts, we can develop a deeper understanding of our beliefs, be inspired by the lives and teachings of those who have gone before us and grow in our relationship with God. Spiritual reading allows us to connect with the rich tradition of our faith, drawing upon the experiences and insights of those who have sought to live out their beliefs in a meaningful and transformative way.

As we reflect on the importance of spiritual reading, it is essential to consider how this practice can enrich our spiritual lives. Whether we are delving into Scripture, exploring the writings of the saints, or engaging with contemporary spiritual authors, we are invited to open our hearts and minds to the wisdom and guidance that these works have to offer.

Questions:

❖ How does spiritual reading enrich your spiritual life?

_____
_____
_____

❖ What books or writings have had the greatest impact on your faith?

_____
_____
_____

❖ How can you make spiritual reading a more consistent part of your daily routine?

_____
_____
_____

❖ Are there any specific topics or areas of your faith that you would like to explore through spiritual reading?

_____
_____
_____

❖ How can you share the insights and wisdom you gain through spiritual reading with others?

_____
_____
_____

Actions:

As you reflect on the importance of spiritual reading in your spiritual life, consider the following five suggestions informed by Catholic social teachings.

These suggestions are intended to guide and inspire you in your journey rather than prescribe a specific course of action.

- ❖ Choose a spiritual book or religious text to read and reflect on during the remainder of Lent. This can be a classic work, a contemporary book, or even a collection of essays or articles on a specific topic.

- ❖ Set aside a dedicated time each day for spiritual reading, even if it's just for 15 minutes. Consistency is key in making this practice a regular part of your spiritual life.

- ❖ Join a spiritual book club or discussion group, either in person or online. Engaging in conversation with others about your spiritual reading can offer new insights and deepen your understanding of the material.

- ❖ Reflect on how your spiritual reading has impacted your faith and relationship with God. Consider writing in a journal or sharing your thoughts with a trusted friend or spiritual advisor.

- ❖ Share the fruits of your spiritual reading with others by recommending books or writings that have been particularly meaningful to you. This can be a simple way to encourage others in their spiritual journey.

In the space provided below, write your answers and reflections on these suggestions. Remember, this is a personal journey, and your responses will help you grow and deepen your understanding of the importance of spiritual reading in your spiritual life.

_____

_____

_____

_____

_____

_____

As we conclude Day 32 of our spiritual journey together, I hope that you have found inspiration and encouragement in exploring the importance of spiritual reading. This practice offers us a wealth of wisdom, guidance, and connection to the rich tradition of our faith. By committing to regular spiritual reading, we can deepen our understanding of our beliefs, grow in our relationship with God, and be inspired by the examples of those who have gone before us.

As you continue to nurture your faith through spiritual reading, may you experience the joy and peace that comes from connecting with the wisdom of our spiritual ancestors and opening your heart to the transformative power of their words. Tomorrow, we will embark on another day of spiritual exploration and growth, and I eagerly look forward to sharing that journey with you. Remember how far you have come in this journey, and embrace the spiritual growth that awaits you in the days to come.

Day 33: The Power of Intercessory Prayer

Welcome to Day 33 of our spiritual journey together. As we continue to grow and deepen our faith, today we will explore the power of intercessory prayer. This form of prayer, in which we pray for the needs of others, is a beautiful expression of our love and compassion for those around us. By lifting others up in prayer, we join in their struggles and joys, and we participate in the transformative power of God's love and grace.

St. Monica's Prayer for the Conversion of Loved Ones is a fitting example of the power of intercessory prayer. St. Monica, the mother of St. Augustine, prayed for her son's conversion for many years, and her prayers were ultimately answered when he became one of the Church's greatest theologians and saints. Her persistent prayer demonstrates the importance of never giving up on our loved ones and trusting in the power of God's love to change hearts and lives.

Reflection:

Intercessory prayer is a vital aspect of our spiritual lives. When we pray for others, we open our hearts to God's love and mercy, allowing it to flow through us and touch the lives of those for whom we pray. This selfless act of prayer not only benefits those we pray for but also deepens our own relationship with God.

In the Gospels, Jesus encourages us to pray for one another, and throughout history, countless saints have modelled the importance of intercessory prayer in their own lives. By following their example, we participate in a long-standing tradition of faith and love.

When we engage in intercessory prayer, we also acknowledge our interconnectedness with others. We recognise that we are all part of the same human family, bound together by our shared faith, hope, and love. This awareness can help us to develop a greater sense of empathy and compassion for others as we come to see their struggles and joys as our own.

Moreover, intercessory prayer has the power to bring about real change in the lives of those for whom we pray. While we may not always see the results of our prayers immediately, we can trust that God hears our prayers and works in mysterious ways to bring about His will in the lives of those we lift in prayer.

Questions:

❖ How has intercessory prayer played a role in your spiritual life so far?

_____

_____

_____

❖ Can you recall a time when someone's intercessory prayers had a positive impact on your life or the life of someone you know?

_____

_____

_____

❖ What challenges do you face when engaging in intercessory prayer, and how can you overcome these obstacles?

_____

_____

_____

❖ How do you feel when you know someone is praying for you or your loved ones?

_____

_____

_____

❖ In what ways can you be more intentional in your practice of intercessory prayer?

_____

_____

_____

Actions:

Make a list of people in your life who need prayer. Consider friends, family members, co-workers, and even strangers you may have encountered.

Write their names here:

_____

_____

_____

Commit to praying for these individuals daily. Set aside a specific time and place to pray for them and be consistent in your practice.

If possible, let the people you are praying for know that you are lifting them in prayer. This simple act can provide comfort and encouragement to those in need.

Seek out opportunities to participate in group intercessory prayer, whether in your local parish or through online prayer groups.

Reflect on your own experiences of being prayed for by others. How has this support impacted your life, and how can you extend this same support to others?

As we conclude Day 33, I hope that you have been inspired to explore the power of intercessory prayer in your own spiritual journey. Remember that praying for others is an essential part of our call to love one another and to participate in the transformative power of God's love and grace.

As we look forward to tomorrow, let us be mindful of the many people in our lives who need our prayers, and let us commit to lifting them with love, faith, and hope. This practice will not only enrich their lives but also strengthen our own relationship with God and deepen our sense of empathy and compassion for others.

May your journey through these days of Lent continue to be a time of growth, self-discovery, and spiritual renewal. Let us thank God for the gift of prayer and the countless ways it can draw us closer to Him and one another.

Day 34: The Call to Holiness

As we continue our Lenten journey, today's focus is on the universal call to holiness. It's an invitation that God extends to every one of us, regardless of our background, vocation, or circumstances in life. It can be daunting to consider the idea of becoming a saint but remember that saints are ordinary people who choose to respond to God's grace in extraordinary ways. Through prayer, self-sacrifice, and love for others, they became models of Christian living and examples of God's transformative power at work in the world.

Let us begin our reflection today with the beautiful prayer of St. Thérèse of Lisieux, a saint known for her simplicity and her "Little Way" of pursuing holiness through everyday acts of love and sacrifice.

Prayer:

St. Thérèse of Lisieux's Prayer to Be a Saint

O my God! I offer Thee all my actions of this day for the intentions and for the glory of the Sacred Heart of Jesus. I desire to sanctify every beat of my heart, my every thought, my simplest works, by uniting them to Its infinite merits; and I wish to make reparation for my sins by casting them into the furnace of Its Merciful Love.

O my God! I ask of Thee for myself and for those whom I hold dear, the grace to fulfill perfectly Thy Holy Will, to accept for love of Thee the joys and sorrows of this passing life, so that we may one day be united together in heaven for all Eternity.

Amen.

Reflection:

In our reflection today, let's ponder how we are called to grow in holiness. Sometimes we might feel overwhelmed by the notion of becoming a saint or even believe that holiness is reserved for a select few. However, the reality is that every single one of us is called to sanctity, and it begins with a personal response to the invitation of Jesus to follow Him and be transformed by His love.

When we think of holiness, we might imagine grand gestures, great acts of charity, or extraordinary acts of faith. But the truth is that holiness can be found in the ordinary, everyday moments of life. It is in the small acts of kindness, the quiet moments of prayer, and the daily sacrifices we make for others that we encounter the presence of God and grow in our relationship with Him.

As you reflect on your own spiritual journey, consider the following questions:

❖ How do you respond to the call to holiness in your life?

_____

_____

_____

❖ In what ways can you grow in holiness?

_____

_____

_____

- ❖ What are some of the obstacles that hold you back from embracing the call to holiness?

  _____

  _____

  _____

- ❖ How can you draw inspiration from the lives of the saints to help you grow in sanctity?

  _____

  _____

  _____

- ❖ How can you make space for God's grace to work in your life and guide you towards holiness?

  _____

  _____

  _____

In today's action step, think about one area in your life where you need spiritual growth. Perhaps you struggle with patience, humility, or forgiveness. Maybe you find it difficult to make time for prayer or to serve others. Whatever the area, create a plan to work on it, trusting that God will provide the grace and strength needed to help you grow in holiness.

Some suggestions for growth inspired by Catholic social teachings include:

- ❖ Volunteering your time to serve the poor or marginalised in your community.

- ❖ Making a conscious effort to practice forgiveness and reconciliation with someone you've been struggling with.

- ❖ Engaging in regular spiritual reading to deepen your understanding of your faith.

- ❖ Participating in a faith-sharing group to build community and grow in your relationship with God.

- ❖ Adopting a consistent prayer routine to cultivate a deeper connection with God.

In the space provided below, write your answers and reflections on these suggestions. Remember, this is a personal journey, and your responses will help you grow and deepen your understanding of the importance of spiritual reading in your spiritual life.

_____

_____

_____

_____

_____

_____

As we conclude our reflection today, remember that the journey to holiness is a lifelong process. We are all works in progress, and God's grace is always available to help us grow and transform. Let us be encouraged by the example of the saints and trust that, with God's help, we can answer the call to holiness in our own lives.

As we look forward to tomorrow, let us continue to seek the guidance of the Holy Spirit and open our hearts to the transformative power of God's love. Together, let's strive to grow in holiness and become the people God has created us to be.

Day 35: The Power of Forgiveness

As we journey further into Lent today, we reflect on the power of forgiveness. Forgiveness is a gift we give to ourselves and others, releasing the burden of resentment and opening the door to healing and reconciliation. In our relationships and interactions, forgiveness is a critical component of our spiritual growth, allowing us to extend the same mercy and compassion that God shows us.

Prayer:

O God, author of innocence and lover of chastity, who bestowed the grace of martyrdom on your handmaid, the Virgin Saint Maria Goretti, in her youth, grant, we pray, through her intercession, that, as you gave her a crown for her steadfastness, so we, too, may be firm in obeying your commandments. – The Roman Missal

Reflection:

In our reflection today, let's delve into the healing power of forgiveness and its significance in our spiritual lives. Forgiveness is not always easy, and at times, it can feel impossible. Yet, when we hold on to grudges, bitterness, and anger, we are the ones who suffer. In contrast, forgiveness brings freedom and peace, allowing us to grow in love and understanding.

Jesus himself taught us the importance of forgiveness, both in his words and actions. He forgave those who persecuted him, and he urged us to forgive others "not seven times, but seventy-seven times" (Matthew 18:22). By practising forgiveness, we are aligning ourselves with the heart of God, who is always ready to forgive and embrace us with open arms.

As you ponder the role of forgiveness in your spiritual journey, consider the following questions:

❖ How has forgiveness played a role in your spiritual journey?

❖ How can you practice forgiveness more fully?

❖ Can you recall a time when you struggled to forgive someone? What helped you eventually let go and forgive?

❖ How can you better accept God's forgiveness for your own shortcomings and sins?

❖ What steps can you take to help others experience forgiveness and healing?

Action:

In today's action step, think about a situation in which you need to forgive or seek forgiveness. Perhaps there is a strained relationship or unresolved conflict that weighs heavily on your heart. Take the necessary steps toward reconciliation, trusting that God will provide the strength and grace needed for healing.

Some suggestions for practising forgiveness inspired by Catholic social teachings include:

- ❖ Praying for the person who has hurt you or whom you have hurt, asking God to bless and heal them.

- ❖ Engaging in a conversation with the person involved, seeking to understand their perspective and respectfully sharing your own feelings.

- ❖ Participating in the Sacrament of Reconciliation to experience God's forgiveness and mercy.

- ❖ Reflecting on the Parable of the Prodigal Son (Luke 15:11-32) to remind yourself of God's boundless love and forgiveness.

- ❖ Practising empathy and compassion by putting yourself in the shoes of the person you need to forgive or seek forgiveness from.

In the space provided below, write your answers and reflections on these suggestions. Remember, this is a personal journey, and your responses will help you grow and deepen your understanding of the importance of spiritual reading in your spiritual life.

_____
_____
_____
_____
_____

As we conclude today's reflection, let us remember that forgiveness is a powerful force for healing and transformation. It enables us to release the past and embrace a future filled with hope, love, and compassion. May we continue to seek God's guidance and grace as we strive to forgive others and accept God's forgiveness for ourselves.

Looking ahead to tomorrow, let us continue our Lenten journey with open hearts and minds, ready to encounter God's love and mercy anew. Be encouraged by how far you have come in this journey, and remain open to the transformative power of forgiveness in your life.

Day 36: The Gift of Faith

Today, as we continue our journey through Lent, we turn our focus to the gift of faith. Our faith is the foundation of our spiritual life and an essential element of our relationship with God.

Prayer:

St. Thomas the Apostle, patron of those seeking faith,

You once doubted the Resurrection of our Lord Jesus Christ,

Until He revealed Himself to you and confirmed your faith.

Help us, in our moments of doubt and uncertainty,

To seek the truth and the guidance of the Holy Spirit.

Strengthen our faith and lead us to a deeper relationship with God.

When we are faced with challenges and questions,

Inspire us to turn to Jesus, our Risen Lord,

And trust in His infinite love and wisdom.

Grant us the grace to persevere in our faith,

To grow in understanding, and to live by God's Word.

St. Thomas the Apostle, pray for us,

That our faith may deepen and our hearts be filled with trust.

Amen

Reflection:

Faith is a deeply personal and transformative aspect of our spiritual lives. It is the source of our hope, guiding us through times of trial and uncertainty. In moments of doubt, it is faith that reminds us of God's unwavering love and presence. Through faith, we are invited to trust in the unseen and believe in the power of God's grace.

Throughout the scriptures, we see the importance of faith. Jesus often tells those he heals, "Your faith has saved you" (Luke 7:50, 8:48). St. Paul tells us that "faith is the assurance of things hoped for, the conviction of things not seen" (Hebrews 11:1). By nurturing our faith, we open ourselves to experiencing the fullness of God's love and presence in our lives.

As you consider the role of faith in your spiritual journey, reflect on these questions:

❖ How does faith sustain you in your spiritual journey?

_____

_____

_____

❖ In what areas of your life do you need to strengthen your faith?

_____

_____

_____

❖ Can you recall a time when your faith was tested? How did you respond, and what did you learn from that experience?

_____

_____

_____

❖ How can you deepen your relationship with God through faith?

_____

_____

_____

❖ What spiritual practices or resources help you grow in faith?

_____

_____

_____

Action:

In today's action step, dedicate time to prayer, asking God to increase your faith. Trust that God is always present and eager to help you grow in your relationship with Him.

Some suggestions for nurturing your faith, informed by Catholic social teachings, include:

❖ Participating in the Sacrament of Reconciliation to experience God's mercy and forgiveness, strengthening your faith in His love.

❖ Attending Mass regularly to be nourished by the Eucharist and the Word of God.

❖ Joining a faith-sharing group or Bible study to deepen your understanding of the scriptures and grow in faith with others.

❖ Practising Lectio Divina, a prayerful reading of scripture, to engage with God's Word and listen for His voice.

❖ Serving others in your community, seeing Christ in those in need and witnessing the transformative power of faith in action.

In the space provided below, write your answers and reflections on these suggestions. Remember, this is a personal journey, and your responses will help you grow and deepen your understanding of the importance of spiritual reading in your spiritual life.

_____
_____
_____
_____
_____
_____

As we conclude today's reflection, let us be grateful for the gift of faith and its role in our spiritual lives. May we continue to nurture our faith and trust in God's love and presence, even when faced with challenges and uncertainties.

As we look forward to tomorrow, be encouraged by your progress on this Lenten journey and remain open to the growth and transformation that faith can bring. Embrace the invitation to strengthen your faith and deepen your relationship with God as you continue this path.

Day 37: The Fruit of the Spirit

As we continue our Lenten journey, today we reflect on the Fruit of the Spirit. These nine qualities, as listed by St. Paul in Galatians 5:22-23, are love, joy, peace, patience, kindness, goodness, faithfulness, gentleness, and self-control. They are the outward signs of the Holy Spirit working within us, transforming our hearts and lives to be more like Christ.

Let us begin our reflection today with a prayer, asking for the grace to cultivate the Fruit of the Spirit in our lives.

Reflection:

Cultivating the Fruit of the Spirit is an ongoing process that requires our cooperation with God's grace. As we open ourselves to the Holy Spirit, we allow Him to transform us from the inside out. The Fruit of the Spirit becomes evident in our actions, words, and attitudes, reflecting the love and presence of God in our lives.

Each fruit has a particular significance and importance in our spiritual journey, as they help us grow in holiness and draw us closer to God. As we reflect on these fruits, consider which ones resonate with you the most and how you can nurture their growth in your life.

Questions:

- ❖ Which fruit of the Holy Spirit resonates with you the most, and why?

_____

_____

❖ How can you nurture the growth of these fruits in your life?

_____
_____
_____

❖ In what ways do you see the Fruit of the Spirit evident in your actions, words, and attitudes?

_____
_____
_____

❖ How does growing in the Fruit of the Spirit impact your relationships with others?

_____
_____
_____

❖ How can you invite the Holy Spirit to work more deeply in your life?

_____
_____
_____

Action:

Choose one Fruit of the Spirit to focus on and practice throughout the day. Be intentional in your efforts to cultivate this fruit and invite the Holy Spirit to guide you.

Some suggestions for nurturing the Fruit of the Spirit in your life, informed by Catholic social teachings, include:

- ❖ Participate in a service project or volunteer opportunity, putting love and kindness into action.

- ❖ Foster peace and reconciliation in your relationships by seeking forgiveness and offering forgiveness to others.

- ❖ Engage in spiritual practices, such as daily prayer, Mass, or adoration, to grow in faithfulness and deepen your relationship with God.

- ❖ Practice patience and gentleness in your interactions with others, recognising the dignity of each person.

- ❖ Cultivate self-control through fasting, abstinence, or other forms of personal sacrifice during Lent.

In the space provided below, write your answers and reflections on these suggestions. Remember, this is a personal journey, and your responses will help you grow and deepen your understanding of the importance of spiritual reading in your spiritual life.

_____

_____

_____

_____

_____

_____

As we conclude today's reflection, let us be mindful of the Fruit of the Spirit at work in our lives. May we continue to be open to the transformative power of the Holy Spirit as we journey through Lent.

As you look forward to the next day, be encouraged by the progress you have made so far and the growth that is taking place in your spiritual life. Continue to cultivate the Fruit of the Spirit and be open to the many ways God is transforming your heart and life.

Day 38: The Joy of Serving Others

As we draw closer to the end of our Lenten journey, today, we explore the joy of serving others. The act of giving ourselves in service to those in need not only brings happiness to those we serve but also nurtures our spiritual growth.

Let us begin today's reflection by offering a prayer for charity, asking God to inspire and guide us in our service to others.

Prayer:

Noble Saint Vincent de Paul,

beloved servant of the poor,

may we follow your example and do good works

among those whom society has abandoned,

enslaved, or forgotten.

Inspire us to feed the hungry,

to love a child,

to provide comfort and medicine to the sick,

to clothe those whose garments are threadbare,

and to offer hope and our Lord's words

to all who need respite.

Pray for us to our beloved God

that we may commit ourselves selflessly

to doing the same charitable acts

that you did all your life,

and intercede with him

that we may have the favour of his guidance

and strength and love upon this important and meaningful work.

Amen.

Reflection:

Service is at the heart of the Christian life, as Jesus himself said, "For even the Son of Man did not come to be served, but to serve, and to give his life as a ransom for many" (Mark 10:45). As followers of Christ, we are called to emulate his example, reaching out to others with love, compassion, and humility.

When we serve others, we encounter Christ in the faces of those we help. This experience brings us closer to God and helps us to grow in our understanding of the dignity and worth of every person. Moreover, service allows us to witness the transformative power of love in action, fostering a deeper appreciation of the Gospel message.

Questions:

❖ How has serving others impacted your spiritual life?

_____

_____

_____

❖ What are some ways you can serve others more fully?

_____

_____

_____

❖ How have you experienced the joy of serving others?

_____
_____
_____

❖ How does serving others deepen your understanding of the Gospel message?

_____
_____
_____

❖ How can you make service a more integral part of your spiritual life?

_____
_____
_____

Action:

Volunteer at a local charity, community centre, or church event. As you serve, be open to the joy that comes from giving of yourself to others.

Here are some suggestions for serving others, informed by Catholic social teachings:

❖ Volunteer at a local food bank or soup kitchen, helping to provide nourishment for those in need.

❖ Offer your time and skills to a homeless shelter, providing support and encouragement to those who are struggling.

❖ Visit a nursing home or hospital, bringing comfort and companionship to the sick and elderly.

- ❖ Engage in advocacy work, using your voice to promote social justice and raise awareness of the needs of the marginalised.

- ❖ Mentor a young person, offering guidance and support as they navigate the challenges of life.

In the space provided below, write your answers and reflections on these suggestions. Remember, this is a personal journey, and your responses will help you grow and deepen your understanding of the importance of spiritual reading in your spiritual life.

_____
_____
_____
_____
_____
_____

As we conclude today's reflection, let us carry the joy of serving others in our hearts. May our service to others be a testament to the love of Christ at work within us and a source of spiritual growth.

As you look forward to the next day, remember how far you have come on this journey and the many ways you have grown spiritually. Be open to the opportunities for service that lie ahead, and let the joy of serving others continue to shape your spiritual life.

Day 39: Preparing for the Resurrection

As we approach the culmination of our Lenten journey today, we focus on preparing our hearts for the joyous celebration of Christ's Resurrection. The Resurrection is the cornerstone of our faith, the event that transformed despair into hope and confirmed the promise of eternal life. Let us begin with a prayer that reflects on the time Jesus spent in the tomb, awaiting the miracle that would change the course of history.

Reflection:

The Resurrection signifies God's triumph over sin and death, a victory that has profound implications for our lives as Christians. As St. Paul reminds us, "If Christ has not been raised, your faith is futile; you are still in your sins" (1 Corinthians 15:17). The Resurrection demonstrates the power of God's love and His promise to never abandon us. Through the Resurrection, we are given the hope of eternal life and the assurance that our own struggles and suffering have meaning and purpose.

Questions:

❖ How does the Resurrection shape your understanding of your faith?

_____

_____

_____

❖ How can you prepare your heart to celebrate the Resurrection?

_____

_____

_____

- ❖ How has your understanding of the Resurrection evolved throughout your spiritual journey?

_____

_____

_____

- ❖ In what ways does the Resurrection bring you hope and comfort?

_____

_____

_____

- ❖ How can you share the joy of the Resurrection with others?

_____

_____

_____

Action:

Meditate on the events of the Passion and Resurrection, considering their personal significance for you. As you reflect, allow the enormity of Christ's sacrifice and the miracle of His Resurrection to touch your heart and deepen your faith.

Here are some suggestions for meditation, informed by Catholic social teachings:

- ❖ Contemplate the depth of Jesus' love for you, demonstrated through His willingness to endure the suffering of the Cross.

- ❖ Reflect on the hope and promise of eternal life that the Resurrection offers to each of us.

- ❖ Consider how the Resurrection can inspire you to live a life of love, compassion, and service.

- ❖ Meditate on the transformational power of the Resurrection and how it can bring new life and renewal to your own spiritual journey.

- ❖ Pray for the grace to share the joy of the Resurrection with others, especially those who are struggling or in need of hope.

In the space provided below, write your answers and reflections on these suggestions. Remember, this is a personal journey, and your responses will help you grow and deepen your understanding of the importance of spiritual reading in your spiritual life.

_____
_____
_____
_____
_____
_____

As we conclude today's reflection, let us carry the hope and promise of the Resurrection in our hearts and let it inspire and guide us in our ongoing spiritual journey. We have come so far on this path, and with the Resurrection as our beacon of light, we can continue to grow in faith, love, and holiness.

As you anticipate the final days of Lent and the celebration of Christ's Resurrection, remember the spiritual progress you have made during this time. Let the joy of the Resurrection fill your heart and embrace the hope it offers as you continue on your journey of faith.

Day 40: Celebrating New Life in Christ

We have now reached the final day of our Lenten journey, and we prepare to celebrate the glorious Resurrection of our Lord Jesus Christ. As we reflect on the past 40 days, let us give thanks for the growth, insights, and transformations we have experienced. With hearts filled with joy, let us come together in prayer, praising God for the miracle of the Resurrection.

Reflection:

The Resurrection is the ultimate expression of God's love for us, a love that conquers death and opens the door to eternal life. As we embrace the joy of the Resurrection, let us also embrace the new life it offers us. This new life is an invitation to deepen our faith, grow in love and service, and share the Good News of Christ's victory with those around us.

Questions:

❖ How has your spiritual journey evolved over the 40 days of Lent?

_____
_____
_____

❖ What lessons have you learned, and how can you carry these insights into the Easter season and beyond?

_____
_____
_____

❖ How has your understanding of the Resurrection deepened during this Lenten journey?

_____

_____

_____

❖ In what ways can you live out the joy of the Resurrection in your daily life?

_____

_____

_____

❖ How can you share the hope and joy of the Resurrection with others, especially those in need?

_____

_____

_____

Action:

Attend Easter Vigil or Easter Sunday Mass and celebrate the Resurrection with your faith community. Reflect on your Lenten journey and commit to continue growing in your faith throughout the year.

Here are some suggestions for action, informed by Catholic social teachings:

❖ Participate in Easter traditions that foster a sense of community and celebrate the joy of the Resurrection.

❖ Reach out to those who may be struggling during the Easter season, offering hope and support through acts of love and kindness.

- ❖ Commit to continued spiritual growth by engaging in regular prayer, spiritual reading, and participation in the sacraments.

- ❖ Find ways to serve your community and promote social justice inspired by the hope and joy of the Resurrection.

- ❖ Share your experience of the Lenten journey with others, encouraging them to explore their own spiritual growth and transformation.

In the space provided below, write your answers and reflections on these suggestions. Remember, this is a personal journey, and your responses will help you grow and deepen your understanding of the importance of spiritual reading in your spiritual life.

_____

_____

_____

_____

_____

As we conclude our 40-day Lenten journey together, let us give thanks for the insights, transformations, and growth we have experienced. As we celebrate the Resurrection of our Lord, let us carry the joy and hope of this miracle into the Easter season and beyond. The journey does not end here; it continues as we strive to live out our faith and share the love of Christ with the world.

May the joy of the Resurrection fill your heart, and may you carry this joy with you as a beacon of hope and love for all to see. Rejoice, for Christ is risen, and through Him, we have been given the gift of new life.

Printed in Great Britain
by Amazon